**THE "BOOK OF" SERIES**
*The Book of Bushido: The Complete Guide to Real Samurai Chivalry*
*The Book of Ninja: The First Complete Translation of the Bansenshukai*
*The Book of Samurai: Fundamental Samurai Teachings* (Book 1)
*The Book of Samurai: Arms, Armour & the Tactics of Warfare* (Book 2)

**THE "ULTIMATE" SERIES**
*The Ultimate Art of War: A Step-by-Step Guide to the Teachings of Sun Tzu*
*The Ultimate Guide to Yin Yang: An Illustrated Exploration of the Chinese Concept of Opposites*

**BOOKS ON SAMURAI, NINJA AND JAPAN**
*How to Be a Modern Samurai: 10 Steps to Finding Your Power and Achieving Success*
*Iga and Koka Ninja Skills: The Secret Shinobi Scrolls of Chikamatsu Shigenori*
*In Search of the Ninja: The Historical Truth of Ninjutsu*
*Modern Ninja Warfare: Tactics and Methods for the Modern Warrior*
*Ninja Skills: The Authentic Ninja Training Manual*
*Old Japan: Secrets from the Shores of the Samurai*
*Samurai and Ninja: The Real Story Behind the Japanese Warrior Myth that Shatters the Bushido Mystique*
*Samurai War Stories*
*Secrets of the Ninja: The Shinobi Teachings of Hattori Hanzo*
*The Dark Side of Japan: Ancient Black Magic, Folklore, Ritual*
*The Lost Samurai School: Secrets of Mubyoshi Ryu*
*The Secret Traditions of the Shinobi: Hattori Hanzo's Shinobi Hiden and other Ninja Scrolls*
*True Path of the Ninja: The Definitive Translation of the Shoninki*

**OTHER BOOKS**
*The Illustrated Guide to Viking Martial Arts*
*The Lost Warfare of India: An Illustrated Guide*

**ON AUDIBLE**
*The Ultimate Art of War: A Step-by-Step Guide to the Teachings of Sun Tzu*
*How to Be a Modern Samurai: 10 Steps to Finding Your Power and Achieving Success*

# THE ULTIMATE
# I CHING

## AN ILLUSTRATED STEP-BY-STEP
## GUIDE TO THE BOOK OF CHANGES

### ANTONY CUMMINS

WATKINS
Sharing Wisdom Since 1893

# THE ULTIMATE I-CHING
## ANTONY CUMMINS

This edition first published in the UK and USA in 2022 by
Watkins, an imprint of Watkins Media Limited
Unit 11, Shepperton House
89–93 Shepperton Road
London N1 3DF

enquiries@watkinspublishing.com

Design and typography copyright © Watkins Media Limited 2022
Text and artwork copyright © Antony Cummins 2022

Commissioning Editor: Fiona Robertson
Managing Editor: Daniel Culver
Editor: James Hodgson
Head of Design: Karen Smith
Design and Typesetting: JCS Publishing Ltd
Production Manager: Uzma Taj

Commissioned Artwork: Jay Kane

A CIP record for this book is available from the British Library.

ISBN: 978-1-78678-651-7 (Hardback)
ISBN: 978-1-78678-729-3 (eBook)

10 9 8 7 6 5 4 3 2 1

Printed in China

www.watkinspublishing.com

# QUICK-FIRE SUMMARY

Before you get started you may find it helpful to refer to the following, which lays out the I-Ching process in simple steps:

1 Formulate a question to ask the universe.

2 Cast your hexagram, using one of the casting methods provided (see pages 62–88).

3 If you have cast any transforming lines, convert them to their opposite to build a second, transformed hexagram (see pages 89–90).

4 Find your original hexagram and transformed hexagram (if you have one) in the chart on page 10.

5 Turn to the section for your original hexagram in Part 2 of this book. Look at the title of the hexagram and the **Read me first** section. If you have no transforming lines, you finish here. If you do have transforming lines, move on to the next step.

6 Look at the individual line commentaries for any transforming lines in your original hexagram.

7 Now turn to the section for your transformed hexagram. Look at the title and the **Read me first** section only. This is the end of your reading.

## ACKNOWLEDGEMENTS

Thanks goes to the following people for supporting me:

Adam Quattlebaum, Alex Hammond, Andrew Ewens, Ben McCarty, Charles Wilk, Cheryl Hillen, Chris Allred, Chris Devincenzi, Christian Ottman, Clarence Sheets, Dan Oftelie, Dennis Milius, Dr C. R. Hughes, Emma Moon, Erich Nolte, Gary Hadley, George Kokonas, Heorhii Zhyvotok, James Cody Kroll, John Hayter, the late Joe Hilen, Jorge Uribe, Justin Root, Kugane Gaming, Kyro Lantsberger, Marcel Pip, Michael Mello, Michael Stephenson, Michael Strauch, Mikael Bergström, Neil Hirst, Nick Mayer, Pablo Martinez, Pär Skoglund, Rene Gysenbergs, Robert Ensign, Robert Shafer, Shaun Burge, Stephen Crump, Steward Barclay, Timo Bammann and Tobe Roberts.

# CONTENTS

# THE I-CHING HEXAGRAM CHART

This is the most important table in the book, which is why it is here – right at the beginning. You will need to refer to it every time you make a casting. Use it to identify the number of the six-line hexagram you have cast so that you can then look up that hexagram in Part 2 to understand what it means.

This book explains the full casting process in detail, but if you just want a quick reminder turn to page 100.

UPPER TRIGRAM

LOWER TRIGRAM

| | | | |
|---|---|---|---|
| 1 | 11 | 34 | 5 |
| 12 | 2 | 16 | 8 |
| 25 | 24 | 51 | 3 |
| 6 | 7 | 40 | 29 |
| 33 | 15 | 62 | 39 |
| 44 | 46 | 32 | 48 |
| 13 | 36 | 55 | 63 |
| 10 | 19 | 54 | 60 |

THE ULTIMATE I-CHING

# UPPER TRIGRAM

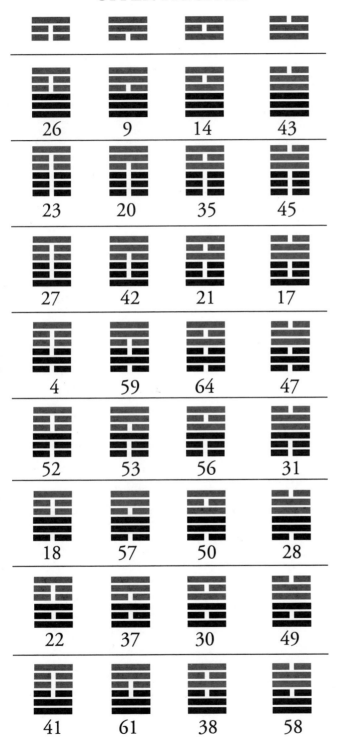

易經

# WAIT, STOP!
# READ THIS FIRST

# WAIT, STOP!
# READ THIS FIRST

Whether you are completely new to the I-Ching or are already well acquainted with the subject, please pause and read this practical introductory section before rushing ahead. It will save you a lot of time and effort, as it has been designed to guide you quickly and easily around the book. Here you will find: an explanation of how far this book goes into the I-Ching and why; a very brief summary of what the I-Ching is and how to use it; and important page numbers to get you directly to where you need to be.

## WHY DO WE NEED THIS VERSION OF THE I-CHING?

There are so many versions of the I-Ching available today, from the extremely academic to the pocket book format. Why then do we need another? The simple answer is that what has been missing until now is a straightforward yet comprehensive guide that respects the original translation but cuts through its complexities.

This book starts from the very beginning and breaks down the complete history, philosophy and method of the I-Ching into sections that will be accessible and relevant to anyone, from total beginner to already competent user. There are many volumes out there which go deeper into the ever-increasing complexity of the manual, but this book is a step-by-step breakdown of everything you need to know to get started. It will take you to a high level of proficiency in the I-Ching from which you can dive into the more advanced texts out there, if you wish to do so.

## THE I-CHING IN A NUTSHELL

Based on an ancient Chinese text of the same name, the I-Ching, or Book of Changes, is a divination tool to help us anticipate changes in our lives and take the most appropriate action.

There are three stages to the I-Ching process:

1. Formulating a question about an issue that you want to understand better
2. Performing a **casting** in order to build a **reading** consisting of either one or two six-line hexagrams
3. Interpreting your reading by letting it resonate within you and also by considering the relevant commentary or commentaries in Part 2 of this book (page 102)

## THE CHINESE CHARACTERS FOR THE I-CHING

The two Chinese characters used to write the I-Ching are 易經. The first character, "i" or "yi" (易), can be summed up as "changes". This can be in the sense of trouble arising or the responses needed to deal with the flow of life. The second character, "jing" or "ching" (經), refers to a book that is held in great respect. Together, they can be taken to mean "a piece of respected or holy literature about the subject of change", but they are normally translated as "Book of Changes" for short. Do not let any connotations from different translations cloud your mind. Always refer back to the original characters and reflect on the I-Ching as a book of deep wisdom that shows us the changes lying ahead of us.

I-Ching

The two Chinese characters that make up the title I-Ching.

## A BRIEF OUTLINE OF CASTING

Casting is at the heart of the I-Ching process. It involves building a hexagram, which is a simple diagram consisting of six horizontal lines. Each of these lines is either solid (—) or broken (– –). There are two main casting methods – using coins or stalks – both of which are fully explained in this book. Simply pick the casting method you want to follow and turn directly to the relevant page, as given below.

### Casting with coins

Casting with coins is the simpler and more common method. To set off now and perform a full coin casting turn to page 64.

### Casting with stalks

Casting with stalks is more complex and takes longer. Although coin casting is more popular these days, some people prefer to follow the ancient tradition of stalk casting because it gives them more time to meditate on their question and they feel a closer connection to the universe. A good way to understand the method is to watch a demonstration video online or, better still, see someone doing it in the flesh. However, this book provides a fully illustrated, step-by-step explanation of the process. If you want to cast with stalks turn to page 69.

### Transforming lines

Each of the six lines in the hexagram you cast will be either solid or broken, and each of these lines will be either static or transforming. Transforming lines change into their opposite; so, a solid line transforms into a broken line and vice versa. If there any transforming lines in the hexagram you have cast, you will need to draw a new, transformed hexagram next to the original one. The original hexagram represents your current situation and the transformed one represents your future situation.

Find the number of each hexagram in the chart on page 10 and then turn to the reading for each number. First look at the reading for your original hexagram, the one that focuses on your situation now. Pay attention to the title and the **Read me first** section, then read *only* about the transforming lines. After this move on to the reading for the transformed hexagram, which shows you the way you need to change to make the correct decisions for the future, and focus on the title and the **Read me first** section only.

The full teaching on this part is found on page 89.

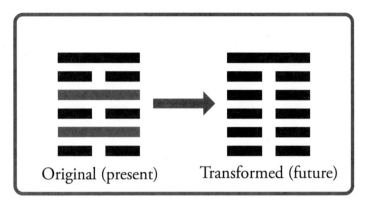

Original (present)    Transformed (future)

Transforming lines are identified in different ways. Sometimes they have a mark next to them or a cross through them; in this book they are shown in red. In the transformed hexagram each transforming line becomes its opposite, but the rest stay the same. This is one of the most important aspects of the I-Ching.

## UNDERSTANDING YOUR READING

There are many ways to understand your reading, but the primary thing to know is that it is not a direct prediction nor will it tell you what to do. What it can do is suggest changes you might make to help you steer a better course. Imagine it as a shining golden thread for you to grasp, helping you find your way out of the "fog" of a situation.

- **If you get a hexagram with no transforming lines:** this is your answer. Look up your hexagram reading using the chart on page 10. Pay attention to general hexagram statement in the **Read me first** section and to the commentaries on all the lines. Because there is no second hexagram all you need to know is here.
- **If you get transforming lines:** focus your attention on the **Read me first** section but then look at only the transforming lines (not the static ones). Only the transforming lines are relevant to you. The next thing to do is look at the transformed hexagram and find your way forward to a new situation.

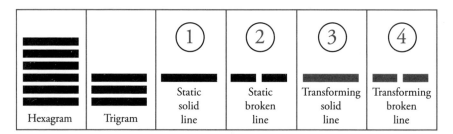

The six basic components of the I-Ching: hexagrams, trigrams and the four types of line. There are eight trigrams, which can be paired up in 64 different ways. These 64 permutations are the hexagrams that form the basis of the I-Ching.

## HOW TO USE THIS BOOK

The first thing to say is that the I-Ching is not a book to read from cover to cover. It is pointless to sit and read each of the hexagrams and their commentaries from 1 to 64. If you already know how to make a casting, you could turn directly to Part 2 of this book and refer to the specific hexagram(s) you have been given.

However, you may wish to raise your understanding of the I-Ching to a new level by finding out more about its history and deeper meanings, as well as the fascinating and complex connections between hexagrams. If so, you will also find some of this information in the first two chapters of Part 1.

If you are totally new to the I-Ching then, as a minimum, you will first need to read all the instructions on casting and reading in the third chapter of Part 1 (on pages 45–101), but then you will join that select group of people who can use this valuable tool to help themselves and their friends navigate their lives. Welcome to the I-Ching.

**Do not worry if this is your first time using the I-Ching and not everything makes sense yet. Things will become clearer as the explanation develops.**

## HOW TO PRONOUNCE AND WRITE I-CHING

Until the second half of the 20th century Chinese characters were rendered in the Roman alphabet using the Wade-Giles system, named after the two British diplomats and sinologists who developed it in the 19th century. However, in the 1950s the Chinese government developed their own system called Pin Yin and made it official. Over recent decades there has been a slow change from the old system to the new. For example, "Taoism" in Wade-Giles has become "Daoism" in Pin Yin, and "Sun Tzu" has become "Sunzi". They are the same words; it is just that there are two ways of writing them.

"I-Ching" is actually the Wade-Giles version. The official Pin Yin version is "Yijing". This is closer to the correct pronunciation, which is something like "eee-ching", "yee-ching" or "yee-jing" rather than "eye-ching" as it is often mispronounced in the west. In this book the more familiar "I-Ching" spelling has been retained, but you should still try to use the correct pronunciation.

# PART ONE

# UNDERSTANDING

# THE I-CHING

The first part of this book tells you the what, why, when and how of the I-Ching. The first chapter traces the historical development of the tradition, from cracks on bones to apps on phones. The second chapter explores the philosophical and spiritual concepts that underpin the I-Ching. And the third chapter tells you everything you need to know to perform your own casting and reading with confidence.

易經

# CHAPTER 1

# WHAT IS
# THE I-CHING?

# WHAT IS THE I-CHING?

The I-Ching starts its history in ancient China, even before the written word was fully developed. Spirit-talkers would communicate with gods and ancestors by burning animal bones and observing the cracks produced. These cracks are believed to be the origin of the I-Ching system of solid and broken lines. As Chinese culture progressed and became more complex, so too did the I-Ching. Eventually, it evolved from an oral tradition into a written collection of 64 hexagrams (*gua*) made up of a total of 384 lines (*yao*), with each hexagram and each individual line having its own connotation. In this chapter we will trace this progression.

## WHAT DOES THE I-CHING ACTUALLY DO?

The spiritual answer to this question is that the I-Ching connects you to ancestor spirits, which in turn connect you to the universe. It is a way to have a conversation with the dead, or with the spirit of the universe or with the creator of all existence, depending on what you believe. The I-Ching is a divine book and it is for holy communication.

A more practical way of approaching this question is to say that when you are in a situation where you do not know the way forward and you need to know which actions or changes to make in your life to progress, then the I-Ching can point you toward the answers.

**Regardless of your own religious beliefs, using the I-Ching is a way to talk to the power that formed the universe.**

## THE ORIGINS OF THE I-CHING

Stretching back into prehistory, the "Chinese" were a collection of many different ethnicities, cultures and belief systems. Within all of the wonderful and dreadful aspects of prehistorical China divination played its part, as it did in all cultures, and the I-Ching was just one of many different forms of divination to have come out of ancient China. Prediction is a fundamental aspect of the human condition. People from all times and places have asked whether there is something beyond our understanding and whether this something *can* or *will* help us.

## ORACLE BONES

Long before the I-Ching came into being, the ancient Chinese would attempt to communicate with the divine by burning so-called oracle bones or shells, typically the shoulder blade of a large mammal or the shell of a turtle.

It is believed that the tribe's spirit-talker would ask a pair of opposing questions, such as:

1   Will X be effective?

2   Will X not be effective?

Multiple tests would be performed over these questions as the bone or shell was cast into flames or scorched until it cracked. The spirit-talker would receive an answer by interpreting the crack lines. It is thought that a solid line signified a "yes" and a broken line signified a "no", but the precise details of these rituals have been lost to history.

## FROM BONES TO HEXAGRAMS

The process by which the I-Ching evolved from marks on oracle bones to the formal system that we still use today spanned many centuries. It is traditionally believed to have been developed in the following stages by three key figures – Fuxi, King Wen and the Duke of Zhou – although much of this story is shrouded in myth.

### Fuxi makes the trigrams

The eight trigrams (*bagua*) upon which the I-Ching is based appear to have been widespread throughout ancient eastern culture and have a mythical origin story. According to the most common story, over 3,500 years ago a legendary snake–human hybrid named Fuxi observed the patterns of the world on a turtle shell as the turtle climbed out of a river. These inspired him to record the eight trigrams.

## King Wen forms the hexagrams

Just over 3,000 years ago, King Wen, the honorary founder of the Zhou dynasty, was imprisoned during the insurgent Zhou dynasty's war with the incumbent Shang dynasty. While in captivity, he is said to have written out the 64 hexagrams in a sequence and given each hexagram a name and a general description. This arrangement is known as the Zhouyi. It is possible that King Wen recomposed the order of the I-Ching from an earlier tradition rather than creating it himself. Further uncertainty is cast by recent archaeological finds that tell us there were other versions of the Zhouyi with the hexagrams arranged in a different order, so no one can be sure what the original format was. However, the sequence we use today has been the accepted text for more than 2,000 years.

## The Duke of Zhou adds the *yao* sentences

A little later the Duke of Zhou, one of the sons of King Wen, wrote down a sentence for each of the six lines in each of the 64 hexagrams and gave each line a name. When King Wen's hexagrams were combined with the Duke of Wen's sentences the I-Ching came fully to life.

### OTHER EARLY I-CHING MANUALS

We know of two other I-Ching manuals – the Lian Shanyi and the Gui Zangyi – both of which predate the Zhouyi, but their contents have been lost. The Lian Shanyi, meaning "Linking Mountains", is also known as the Xiayi as it was created under the Xia dynasty; while the Gui Zangyi, or "Restored to Earth", can also be known as the Shangyi as it dates from the Shang dynasty. One theory is that the primary names for these two manuals are based on the first hexagrams within their sequences. This has led some scholars to speculate that the Zhouyi may not be thus called because it was made during the Zhou dynasty but because the word "zhou" also means "to be prepared" or "to contemplate". It is not important for you to know about this, but it gives an insight into the many competing theories about the I-Ching that academics continue to discuss.

## A TALE OF TWO DYNASTIES?

When we use the I-Ching to perform a casting and get a reading, we look only at the pages relating to the one or two hexagrams that the universe has given us. So, we normally treat each of the 64 hexagrams as an individual entity with no connection to the other 63 hexagrams.

However, some modern commentators on the I-Ching see a definite pattern to the arrangement of the hexagrams in the Zhouyi. They read the hexagrams from number 1 all the way to number 64 as a story of constant change. According to one theory, the 64 hexagrams constitute a historical record of the conflict between the Shang and Zhou dynasties during which the Shang fell and the Zhou rose. This is a significant – albeit contested – aspect of the history and study of the I-Ching, but this book is more concerned with the book's use as a form of divination.

**The I-Ching comes from the very distant past. There are multiple theories for its origin.**

# COMMENTARIES ON THE I-CHING

The original I-Ching was a simple divination manual, but over the centuries various layers of explanatory writings have attached themselves to this pocket book of changes. We owe our understanding of the I-Ching today to these works by specialists in ancient Chinese language and culture.

### ANCIENT COMMENTARIES

The first commentaries, known collectively as the Zhuan, date from around 500 BC, which was already five centuries after the Zhouyi was created. By this time the I-Ching had become established as one of the Five Classics of ancient Chinese wisdom and would almost certainly have been a significant influence on major scholars such as Confucius and Lao

Tzu, author of the Dao De Jing. Viewed in this light, the I-Ching can be seen as a cornerstone of Chinese culture and identity.

The most important ancient work on the I-Ching is the Ten Wings, traditionally attributed to Confucius himself (although this, like so many other aspects of early I-Ching history, is disputed). Many editions of the I-Ching also contain the Ten Wings, either in full or in part.

## The Ten Wings

Legend has it that the sage Confucius (c. 551–479 BC) wrote a series of commentaries on the I-Ching known as the Ten Wings (Shi Yi). They are called "wings" because they are designed to lift the reader up to a better understanding of the I-Ching (in Chinese "wings" can mean "assistance"). In reality, it is more likely that multiple Confucian scholars developed the commentaries over time, bringing their own ideas to bear on the Daoist foundation of the I-Ching.

There are actually seven main commentaries, not ten, but some of them are divided into subsections. The seven main commentaries are:

1   **Dazhuan** – the Great Commentary: an analysis of change within the I-Ching

2   **Shuoguazhuan** – an analysis of the trigrams and their meanings

3   **Xiangzhuan** – an analysis of each hexagram in terms of the position of the lines and trigrams and what they mean

4   **Tuanzhuan** – a Confucian interpretation of the hexagrams with a focus on *yin* and *yang* positions and Confucian morality

5   **Xuaguazhuan** – an analysis of the hexagram sequence (includes the story of King Wen)

6   **Zaguazhuan** – an analysis of the relationships between connected hexagrams (e.g. hexagrams that are inverted versions of each other)

7 **Wenyanzhuan** – an analysis of the first two hexagrams and their connection to the upper and lower canons and also how progression is seen in the I-Ching

The Ten Wings helped transform the I-Ching from a simple divination tool into a vehicle for Confucian philosophy and morality. The idea they promoted was that you can find stability in your life by following a moral compass. In this book the Ten Wings have not been included in their own right, but they are an important source for the guidance in Part 2.

**The original I-Ching was a book of Daoist divination while the later commentaries were a path to Confucian morality.**

## MODERN COMMENTARIES

Some people only accept the Confucian commentaries as valid, but the explanation of the I-Ching is an ongoing process that does not stop in ancient China. The I-Ching has become a worldwide sensation translated across the world into many languages. In recent times there have been stacks of new commentaries, which should not be dismissed just because they are modern. The ancient commentators may have found the language, characters and connotations of the I-Ching easier to interpret, but on the other hand modern commentators are able to draw upon important archaeological discoveries. These insights may actually give them a better understanding of the origins of the I-Ching than the ancient commentators had. Remember that the Confucian scholars were writing 500 years after the creation of the Zhouyi and perhaps up to 2,000 years after the tradition came into being.

**The ancient commentators may not have always been correct. Modern research can sometimes outdo the old masters.**

# A TIMELINE OF THE I-CHING

This timeline combines major historical events and the key stages in the evolution of the I-Ching in order to give you a clear picture of where the I-Ching fits into Chinese and world history. Note that most of the dates in the ancient part of the timeline are approximate.

**10,000 BC and before**
China is in the Neolithic Period (New Stone Age). The Yangshao culture centred in tribes around the Yellow River uses basic stone tools.

**4000 BC and before**
Around this time humans are building the first towns and even cities and empires, with their power based on the harvesting and control of crops. Nomadic hunter-gatherer culture is beginning to be replaced by agriculture and civilization starts to bloom.

**3500 BC**
Invention of the wheel means that carts can be used to carry heavy loads.

**3000 BC**
The first stages of Stonehenge are laid down: earthworks are dug and timber posts are erected. In China a new society starts to emerge, known as the Longshan or Black Pottery Culture.

**2711 BC**
The Yellow Emperor, or Huangdi, is said to have been born. A semi-legendary man who was later mythologized, he is credited with helping to create the foundations of Chinese society and appears throughout Chinese literature.

**2600 BC**
The famous sarsen stones of Stonehenge are raised and the trilithons stand against the sky.

**2500 BC**
The great pyramid of Giza in Egypt is built. Ancient Egyptian culture is at its height.

## 2500 BC
The mythological deity Fuxi is said to have created the eight trigrams (*bagua*), which represent a basic understanding of nature, landscape and natural phenomena.

## 2100 BC
Rise of the Xia dynasty in China. An early version of the I-Ching known as the Lian Shanyi is developed. Only fragments of it remain – just enough for us to know that it existed.

## 2000 BC
The earliest evidence of Chinese spirit-talkers burning animal bones to divine answers from the ancestors dates from this period.

## 1600 BC
Fall of the Xia dynasty and founding of the Shang dynasty. Some of the divination skills used at this time eventually make their way into the I-Ching. The Shang are the "evil enemy" of the Zhou within I-Ching tradition.

## 1200 BC
The Iron Age develops in what is now Iraq and spreads to other parts of the world.

## 1112 BC
Birth of King Wen, father of the Zhou dynasty and supposed creator of the so-called King Wen sequence of I-Ching hexagrams still used today. The date of his birth is disputed; some scholars give it as 1152 BC.

## 1050 BC
Fall of the Shang dynasty and founding of the Zhou dynasty. The yarrow-stalk method of divination begins to replace the burning of animal bones.

## 1042 BC
The Duke of Zhou adds explanations of each of the 384 lines in the 64 hexagrams drawn out by his father, King Wen. The Zhouyi, the original core of the I-Ching, is now complete.

**776 BC**
The first Olympic Games is thought to have been held.

**571 BC**
Birth of Lao Tzu, author of the Dao De Jing, the foundational text of Daoism.

**551 BC**
Birth of the Chinese sage Confucius, who throughout his life lays down the system which is known today as Confucianism. Legend has it that Confucius wrote the I-Ching commentary known as the Ten Wings.

**500 BC**
Greece is at war with Persia. Ancient Greek culture moves into its classical phase.

**500 BC**
The Iron Age in China develops and metal starts to become more and more important.

**479 BC**
Death of Confucius.

**475 BC**
Beginning of the Warring States Period in China.

**400 BC**
Rise of Buddhism brings a new way of thinking to the area in and around India.

**221 BC**
End of the Warring States Period.

**202 BC**
Fall of the Zhou dynasty and founding of the Western Han dynasty. Around this time a version of the I-Ching is distributed that includes half of the Ten Wings commentary by Confucius.

**200 BC**

Around this time, the Mawangdui version of the I-Ching is written on silk and placed in a tomb. One of the oldest known versions of the I-Ching, it follows a different order from the King Wen sequence.

**85 BC**

A Chinese historian from this time writes that Confucius loved the I-Ching so much he wore the bindings out and attributes the Ten Wings to Confucius, thereby popularizing the connection between the I-Ching and Confucius.

**44 BC**

Assassination of Julius Caesar in Rome by Brutus and companions.

**AD 0**

Birth of Jesus Christ.

**AD 25**

Beginning of the Eastern Han dynasty.

**AD 249**

The Chinese scholar Wang Bi dies and leaves behind influential commentaries of the I-Ching, Dao De Jing and the Analects of Confucius.

**AD 570**

Birth of the Prophet Mohammad.

**AD 618**

Founding of the Tang dynasty. During this period, the three-coin method of the I-Ching becomes more popular than the yarrow-stalk method.

**AD 800**

Scandinavian travellers, raiders and traders start to move about the western world establishing colonies. We know them collectively as the Vikings.

**AD 907**

Fall of the Tang dynasty. China returns to political instability.

**AD 1066**
William the Conqueror invades Britain and becomes the first Norman king of England.

**AD 1100**
The First Crusade comes to an end and the Kingdom of Jerusalem establishes western power in the Middle East.

**AD 1205–1279**
China is ruled by the Mongol Empire.

**AD 1347**
The Black Death sweeps Europe, killing up to 50% of the population.

**AD 1420**
Beginning of the Italian Renaissance.

**AD 1600**
European travellers start to colonize the Americas.

**AD 1760**
Beginning of the Industrial Revolution in England.

**AD 1775**
Beginning of the American Revolution.

**AD 1789**
The French Revolution starts and France overthrows its monarchy.

**AD 1882**
James Legge publishes the first English translation of the I-Ching.

**AD 1899**
German missionary Richard Wilhelm travels to China and falls in love with Chinese culture.

**AD 1911**

Richard Wilhelm starts to study and translate the I-Ching under Master Lao Ni-hsuan.

**AD 1914–1918**

World War I. Richard Wilhelm has to wait for the war to finish before he can complete his translation of the I-Ching.

**AD 1923**

Publication of Wilhelm's German translation of the I-Ching.

**AD 1939–1945**

World War II.

**AD 1950**

The Bollingen Foundation publishes an English translation by Cary Baynes of the I-Ching based on Richard Wilhelm's German version. Renowned psychologist Carl Jung contributes a foreword, which helps to popularize the I-Ching in the English-speaking world.

**AD 1973**

Discovery of the Mawangdui version of the I-Ching.

**AD 2000**

With the explosion of the internet, I-Ching websites, apps and free readings become popular.

**AD 2008**

The Beijing Olympics start at the eighth hour of the eighth day of the eighth month of 2008, a particularly auspicious date and time.

**AD 2023**

*The Ultimate I-Ching* by Antony Cummins is published by Watkins.

# 易經

# CHAPTER 2

# THE POWER BEHIND THE I-CHING

# THE POWER BEHIND THE I-CHING

The Chinese see the I-Ching as a way to communicate with the Dao, the power which created all things. By following the Dao by means of the I-Ching we choose to walk in step with the universe rather than blindly existing without purpose. However, the power behind the I-Ching is only available to those who believe in it. There is no point trying to communicate with the I-Ching if you are not truly listening.

In this chapter, we will learn more about the Dao and the related principle of *yinyang* and how these are embodied in the I-Ching.

## THE DAO: THE POWER BEHIND ALL THINGS

To use the I-Ching you have to believe that messages are really being sent to you through the medium of coins and stalks. If you do not believe that, then the I-Ching has no value to you. But where do these messages come from?

The ancient Chinese believed that when they made a casting of the I-Ching it was their dead ancestors who answered their questions. According to Chinese tradition, spirits of the ancestors, which are called *shen*, meaning "bright ones", remain around the family home to guide living descendants into new times. The I-Ching is one way in which the ghosts of the past can stay with you and guide you to a positive position.

However, ancestral spirits are just a way of personifying the source of the messages delivered via the I-Ching. Ultimately, it is the Dao, the unknowable power behind all things, that is speaking to us.

### WHAT IS THE DAO?

The Dao, or Tao, is the guiding principle behind creation and existence. Represented by the Chinese character for "road" or "way" (道), the Dao is often referred to simply as the Way. According to the ancient Chinese sage Lao Tzu, author of the Dao De Jing, "The Dao that can be named is not the real Dao." He meant by this that the Dao can never truly be understood. All descriptions of the Dao or analogies to convey its essence are only an echo of the truth. As humans, we are caught in three-dimensional space and time, unable to project ourselves beyond the universe or the laws of physics. This means that we cannot know the Dao – but we can still feel its influence.

**The Dao is the indescribable rules of the universe. It was there before the universe existed and it will be there when the universe no longer exists.**

### THE CHINESE THEORY OF CREATION

The traditional Chinese theory of creation is that there was nothing (other than the Dao) until the two forces which humans call *yin* and *yang* began to differentiate from each other. This movement produced *chi*, life force. As the movement continued, *yin chi* and *yang chi* began to combine in increasingly subtle and complex ways to form the "ten thousand things" (萬物), which is the Chinese term used to refer to all of creation. All creations of the universe, from a microbe to a tree to a human being, the sun, moon and planets, the seasons and the weather, are part of this original *yinyang* mix, as are all things that we create and everything we think and feel and do. We are all a part of the Dao, and the Dao is the law that binds the universe in place.

### WHAT IS YINYANG?

*Yinyang* is a single word which represents a pair of contrasting forms of energy. *Yin* and *yang* flow in various ways and make themselves manifest in our world. The snow in winter is *yin*; the heat in summer is *yang*. Things can be *yin* in some contexts and *yang* in others. For example, a glass of cold water is *yin* in relation to a cup of hot tea, but it is *yang* in relation to the ice cube we use to chill the water. Relativity is the key here. *Chi* that is in a state of *yin* moves downward, condenses and forms matter; *chi* in a state of *yang* rises up, expands and animates – gives things their inner spark. Biological females are categorized as being a part of *yin* and biological males as a part of *yang*, but *yin* and *yang* themselves do not have a gender; they are simply forms of energy. In the I-Ching, the broken lines are *yin* and the solid lines are *yang* (although there is more to say on this in the next chapter).

# Yinyang

The Chinese character for *yin* (left) means "shade upon the hill" and the character for *yang* (right) means "sun upon the hill".

An important aspect of *yinyang* theory is that *yin* and *yang* are constantly in flux. Think about the seasons. Midwinter is the time of the year when *yin* is at its most powerful, but it is also the point at which the power of *yin* begins to wane and *yang* begins to regain its strength day by day until it reaches its own peak at midsummer. The I-Ching helps us ride these waves of change and set a course that brings us into harmony with the Way.

(For a complete understanding of the concept of *yinyang* see the book from this series on that subject, *The Ultimate Guide to Yin Yang: An Illustrated Exploration of the Chinese Concept of Opposites*.)

**Yin and yang are contrasting but complementary forms of energy found in all things.**

### OUTSIDE OF TIME AND SPACE

Astrophysicists can tell you how wide the observable universe is, how old it is, what happened within moments of its creation, but they cannot tell you what is "outside" the universe. The laws of physics – of dimension, time and matter – govern the universe, but beyond the universe they do not apply. Beyond the universe there is only the unknowable Dao. The Dao is the rules that hold the universe together, but the Dao is not constrained by the laws of physics. It can observe all timelines, see into your mind, exist beyond the scope of your understanding, and yet it is in everything. You breathe it in and yet it has no substance. These are not the kind of empty paradoxes sometimes dressed up as eastern wisdom; they express a fundamental truth of Chinese philosophy and one that is perhaps not too far removed from the view of modern science.

**The laws of physics are observations of how the Dao manifests itself within the confines of time and space. However, the Dao is both inside and outside the universe; it is before and after the universe as well as during it.**

## IS THE DAO SENTIENT?

Science is the way modern humans understand the creation and operation of the universe. But science has never come close to answering the basic metaphysical question that has occupied humans since the earliest times: what created the universe? As a sentient human facing this question, you have two possibilities to consider: that the universe was created by a creator (no matter what form that takes) or that it came about as the result of a series of physical and chemical processes without design.

If you believe that there was no creator, the I-Ching is not going to be for you. It is therefore assumed that you do believe there is a purpose and agency behind creation. Which leaves you with another two possibilities to consider: that the creator continues to involve itself in our lives or that it created the universe and then left everything to run under a set of rules which we call the laws of physics? Sticking with the Chinese term Dao, which is no better or worse than the term God, does the Dao actively care what we do or did it turn its back on the universe at the moment of creation? This comes down to a question of faith. Viewed purely rationally, one could argue that the rules of the Dao, which have been in place from the start, have the same effect on us whether the Dao is observing us or not. You could see the I-Ching as a means of interacting with a sentient Dao which is passing messages back to you, or you could see it simply as a way to access the programming of the universe. Either way, you have your answer in the form of a hexagram and a reading to follow. This is your message from the universe if you believe it to be so.

**I-Ching readings are messages from the universe. Whether you believe they are personally for you or are stock answers in an ongoing program does not matter. The answer you get is the answer you need.**

# FAITH AND DOUBT

The I-Ching is no different from other systems of divination such as reading tea leaves or the flight of birds or the entrails of sacrificed animals in that it requires a leap of faith on the part of the user. There are just as many reasons – if not more – to doubt what you are being told than to believe in it.

### REASONS TO DOUBT THE I-CHING

Those who are sceptical about the I-Ching might argue that the messages are too vague or mystifying to be interpreted with any confidence. It is certainly true that the original statements accompanying the hexagrams are laden with cultural baggage that is open to interpretation, as are the explanations of individual lines. For example: "Peeling paint from the legs of a bed is a misfortune" (hexagram 23 line 1), or "A duke pays tribute to a ruler; lesser people cannot. Misfortune" (hexagram 14 line 3), or "The waters reach the stairs. Regrets vanish" (hexagram 59 line 2), and so on. What do these mean? Even by the time of Confucius, the original I-Ching was so difficult to penetrate that it had to be reinterpreted in a way that people could understand.

Furthermore, certain combinations of trigrams within hexagrams were interpreted in different, often contradictory ways. For example, a hexagram consisting of the mountain trigram next to the water trigram could be read as a reduction or as a blockage. Thunder next to the heavens could be read as bountiful rain or a looming disaster.

The doubts that some people have are understandable. It is possible that the whole thing is not real. Those people who do not believe in the I-Ching would be better advised to just stop, ask themselves questions and interpret answers in their own way. It is all down to your own beliefs.

### WAYS TO BELIEVE IN THE I-CHING

If you do not believe in the I-Ching, you will not find anything here that will change your mind. This section is about rationalizing the faith people have in the I-Ching rather than converting sceptics. That is why the heading says "ways to believe" not "reasons to believe".

The renowned Swiss psychologist Carl Gustav Jung, who wrote the foreword to the English translation of Richard Wilhelm's German version of the I-Ching, used the term synchronicity to refer to the way believers in the I-Ching attach meaning to apparently randomly generated hexagrams. Jung recognized that the I-Ching relies on the user's belief that the hexagram cast at any particular moment is an indicator of the essential situation prevailing at that time. Synchronicity can be summed up as a coincidence that has meaning.

**Messages from the universe or the unconscious?**
Carl Jung is also well known for his concept of the collective unconscious, which is the idea that people of all cultures are influenced by a set of shared archetypes such as the Hero, the Great Mother and the Wise Old Man passed down through the ages and buried deep in our unconscious. He saw this as an explanation for the similarity of themes to be found in the mythologies of different ancient cultures around the world that would have had no means of communicating with each other at the time.

Some people would argue that the messages delivered by the I-Ching come from within us – not from the "bright spirits" of our ancestors but from our personal relationship to the collective unconscious. This may go against what the ancient Chinese believed, but it can still be a productive way of approaching the I-Ching.

In the end, it does not really matter *how* you believe the I-Ching works so long as you believe that it works.

**Only your scepticism can hinder you. Use the I-Ching with full faith or do not use it at all. The choice is yours.**

易經

# CHAPTER 3

# HOW TO USE THE I-CHING

# HOW TO USE THE I-CHING

The next step in your journey is to learn how to actually use the I-Ching: what the basic building blocks of the system are, what each part means, how the hexagrams are constructed, what kind of question to ask, how to cast a hexagram and, of course, how to read it. There are various different casting methods, some of which may appear more complex than others, but they all achieve the same objective – of building a hexagram that is the answer to your question at a given moment. This chapter will take you step by step through all the different stages in the process.

## APPROACHING THE I-CHING

The I-Ching is a holy book and it should be respected. As previously noted, the term *ching* or *jing* (經) means something akin to "canonical or respected text"; the same character is sometimes used for the Christian Bible. Respecting the I-Ching does not have to involve elaborate rituals; it just means you should save it for when you really need it and pay heed to its message.

### WHEN SHOULD YOU USE THE I-CHING?

It can be tempting to use the I-Ching for every decision, but in many cases you already have the tools within you to make the right choice. In almost all situations there are the things you *want* to do and the things you *should* do. To align yourself with the Dao, only do the things which should be done; be as honest as you can, help other people, do not cause others harm or problems, be true to yourself. To get to the heart of a question, always look at what you want to happen and compare that with what should be done. If in doubt, try reversing the situation and put yourself in the shoes of any other people involved. How would *you* want you to act? This is normally the right answer.

Sometimes the morally correct path is obvious, but in other cases it is less clear. However, even then, pause before consulting the I-Ching. Ask yourself whether you are being honest with yourself. Sometimes when we explain a situation to ourselves we twist our analysis to justify taking the wrong path. If you really cannot see what is best in a situation, only then is it time to take out the I-Ching and ask the universe for guidance.

**Use your own judgement and moral compass to guide you. Only turn to the I-Ching when you genuinely do not know what to do for the best.**

### RESPECTING THE MESSAGE

Some people treat their I-Ching with great reverence; they keep the book and paraphernalia in a sacred space and consider a casting as a ritual to be accompanied with incense, prayers, meditation and silence. This is a valid approach, but it is not the only way. The I-Ching itself does not have to be an object of worship. It is not in itself divine, it is a connection to the divine.

You may already have other copies of the I-Ching, some of which will, no doubt, be epic "door stoppers". However, the original I-Ching was a small document that did not take up much room at all. According to legend, Confucius told his disciples that, because their lives were subject to constant change, they should keep the I-Ching with them at all times. Consider having two copies of the I-Ching, one that you keep clean and cherished at home, the other that you take out with you.

In the end, it does not matter whether your copy of the I-Ching is a beautifully bound volume that you keep on a lectern or a dog-eared paperback that you shove in your pocket, whether you cast with solid gold coins or plastic counters, whether you spend days meditating on your reading or seize on its message in a moment of earnest insight. All that really matters is that you remember who you are "talking" to and that you create time and space to perform your divination with proper intent and respect.

**You do not need to handle your physical copy of the I-Ching with undue reverence, but you do need to respect the message it delivers.**

# ELEMENTS OF THE I-CHING

Just as a dollar can be broken down into cents, dimes and quarters, so the basic currency of the I-Ching, the hexagram, can be broken down into monograms, bigrams and trigrams. Each of these elements is classified as either *yin* or *yang*.

## MONOGRAMS

I-Ching hexagrams are built out of single lines known as monograms ("mono" means "one" and "gram" means "mark"). There are two types of line: solid (—) and broken (– –). In other I-Ching manuals you may find solid lines referred to as *yang* lines and broken lines as *yin* lines.

Solid and broken lines exist in two different states, static and transforming, making a total of four types of line. Static lines are also referred to as young and transforming lines are referred to as old. You might think that it would make more sense for a young line to be transforming and an old line to be static, as youth is commonly associated with growth and old age with stability. However, think of it this way. An old person generally has fewer years left before they die, at which point they will transform into a spirit to continue on their journey; while most young people will not make this transformation for many years and so they are in a more stable state. To avoid any confusion we will use the terms "static" and "transforming" in this book.

There are many ways in which these two states can be represented, including crosses, asterisks, dots and *yinyang* symbols. In this book, static lines are shown in black and transforming lines in red.

All you have to remember is that when you throw the coins or draw the stalks you will get one of these four types of line. You repeat this a total of six times to build your hexagram. Another important thing you need to know is that hexagrams are built from the bottom up. The bottom line is the first to be drawn and the top line is the last (more on this later).

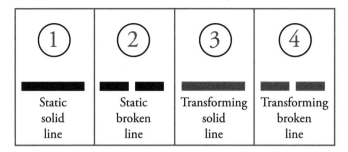

The I-Ching is built on these four types of line:
static solid, static broken, transforming solid and transforming broken.

## BIGRAMS

In other manuals you may find references to bigrams, which are pairs of lines. In the I-Ching system there are four types of bigram and each hexagram consists of three bigrams. However, in this book we will focus on monograms, trigrams and hexagrams, so you will not need to think in terms of bigrams. They are mentioned here just so that you are aware of what they are.

## TRIGRAMS

A single line is a monogram, two lines is a bigram and so it follows that three lines is a trigram. There are eight ways of combining solid and broken lines into a group of three lines. These are the eight trigrams that Fuxi is said to have discerned on the back of a turtle emerging from a river. Each trigram has a meaning and represents an aspect of nature. The following sections will teach you the construction, Chinese name, general translation and meaning for each trigram.

Trigram 1 – Qian

Made up of all *yang* (male) lines, this is the most masculine trigram.

**The Heavens**
*father*

**Qian**
乾

**The Heavens** – In Chinese culture the heavens are seen as masculine and this trigram is made up of three solid *yang* lines, which have male associations. Translations for this trigram include: power, force, will, persistence, strength and creative strength. Its symbol is either the heavens or the dragon and its family association is "father".

---

**MANDATE OF HEAVEN**

The heavens were considered as a holy realm and the rulers of China claimed a divine right to rule, which they called the "mandate of heaven" (*tian ming*).

---

## Trigram 2 – Kun

Made up of all *yin* (female) lines, this is the most feminine trigram.

**Earth** – In Chinese culture the earth is seen as feminine and this trigram is made up of three broken *yin* lines, which have female associations. Translations for this trigram include: nurturing, womb, compassion and field. Its symbol is earth and its family association is "mother".

## Trigram 3 – Zhen

With a *yang* (male) line in the starting position at the bottom, this trigram is associated with the first-born son in a family.

**Thunder** – The thunder trigram also includes lightning by association. Translations for this trigram include: movement, dramatic change, arousal or excitement. Its symbol is thunder or shaking and its family association is "eldest son".

Trigram 4 – Xun

With a *yin* (female) line in the starting position at the bottom, this trigram is associated with the first-born daughter in a family.

**Wind** (or sometimes **Wood**) – While itself invisible, wind has many visible effects. Translations for this trigram include: changing, adaptability, subtlety, flexibility, penetration, the spirit of wood and wind, marriage, and new home. Its symbol is wood or wind and its family association is "eldest daughter".

Note that the Wind trigram is referred to as Wood in some translations. Do not be confused by this. In this book, wind shall be the main term used.

Trigram 5 – Dui

With a *yin* (female) line in the final position at the top, this trigram is associated with the last-born daughter in a family.

**Still Water** – Tranquillity is found in beautiful vistas, which include lakes or other bodies of water where the water is either not moving at all or so slowly that the movement can hardly be perceived. Translations for this trigram include: mist, vapour, celebration, pleasure and stimulation. Its symbol is still water and its family association is "youngest daughter".

### Trigram 6 – Gen

With a *yang* (male) line in the final position at the top, this trigram is associated with the last-born son in a family.

**Mountain** – Sacred places in China, mountains are solid and stable. Translations for this trigram include: mountain spirit, home of the immortal gods, stillness, stopping and serenity. Its symbol is mountain and its family association is "youngest son".

### Trigram 7 – Kan

With a *yang* (male) line rushing through two *yin* (female) lines, this trigram is associated with any middle sons in a family.

**Flowing Water** – Unlike still water (see trigram 5), which is associated with peace, flowing water is a dangerous element, as it brings to mind rushing rapids, treacherous tides, currents and deep gorges. Translations of this trigram include: stream, falling down, rapid flow, hardship, danger and risk. Its symbol is flowing water and its family association is "middle son".

### Trigram 8 – Li

With a *yin* (female) line holding apart two *yang* (male) lines, this trigram is associated with any middle daughters in a family.

Fire – This is one of the most important elements in the ancient world. Translations for this trigram include: radiance, brightness, light, warmth, clarity and clinging together. Its symbol is fire and its family association is "middle daughter".

---

## EARLY COUNTING SYSTEMS

It is believed that in early times people tied knots in strings to record numbers and then may have copied these arrangements of knots on to clay and other markable surfaces. One theory is that these eventually became the lines and dashes that make up the trigrams described here and that the trigrams therefore represent numbers.

---

### Trigram arrangements

Often you will see the trigrams arranged in an octagon. This can be a little confusing, but you just need to be aware that the lines on the outer rim are the top lines and the lines closest to the centre of the octagon are the bottom ones.

There are two different octagonal arrangements: the Earlier Heaven (or Fuxi) arrangement, which positions each trigram opposite its exact inverse; and the Later Heaven (or King Wen) arrangement, which positions each trigram opposite the one that balances it, as seen on the next page.

**You need not worry too much about remembering these arrangements. They are just here to help you understand how the I-Ching came into being.**

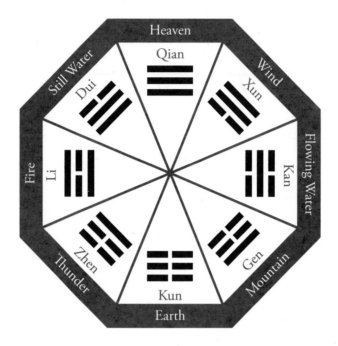

The Earlier Heaven arrangement.

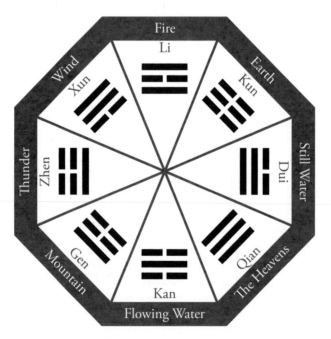

The Later Heaven arrangement.

## The names of the trigrams

For ease of reference, the table below gives the names of the trigrams in both the Wade-Giles and Pin Yin systems (see page 19), as well as in Japanese, which you may also come across in certain commentaries. Note that there are alternative translations for some of the trigrams. Do not become confused by these apparent inconsistencies; they are all part of the tradition.

| Trigram | ☳ | ☴ | ☲ | ☷ | ☱ | ☰ | ☵ | ☶ |
|---|---|---|---|---|---|---|---|---|
| Character | 震 | 巽 | 離 | 坤 | 兌 | 乾 | 坎 | 艮 |
| Wade-Giles | Chen | Sun | Li | K'un | Tui | Ch'ien | K'an | Ken |
| Pin Yin | Zhen | Xun | Li | Kun | Dui | Qian | Kan | Gen |
| Japanese | Shin | Son | Ri | Kon | Da | Ken | Kan | Gon |
| Translation | Thunder | Wind | Fire | Earth | Still Water | The Heavens | Flowing Water | Mountain |
| Other translations | – | Wood | – | – | Marsh Lake | Heaven Sky Dragon | Gorge | – |

### HEXAGRAMS

The six-line hexagram is the base unit of the I-Ching. When you perform a casting, it is a hexagram that you end up with. The hexagram is made up of the lower trigram, which is the bottom three lines (lines 1, 2 and 3), and the upper trigram, which is the top three lines (lines 4, 5 and 6). Like houses, hexagrams are constructed from the bottom up, which is why the line numbering starts at the bottom. Each of the eight trigrams can be paired with itself or one of the other seven trigrams, making a total of 64 different hexagrams.

Remember that each trigram has a meaning, such as "flowing water", "fire", "mountain" and so on. In Chinese thought these represent different states, ideas and situations, which vary according to whether the trigram is in the upper or lower position within the hexagram. For example, fire in the lower position naturally moves up as the flames rise, while water in the upper position naturally moves down.

When studying a hexagram, an I-Ching master will consider how the two trigrams within it relate to each other and how that interaction addresses the question being posed. Broadly speaking, the lower trigram represents the inner world of the questioner, while the upper trigram represents the world around them. While a complex understanding of the relationship between upper and lower trigram is not essential to gain a great understanding of any hexagram, it is an avenue you can take to go deeper into the messages from the universe.

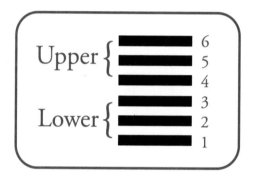

The lower trigram is made up of lines 1, 2 and 3, while the upper trigram is made up of lines 4, 5 and 6.

### YINYANG IN THE I-CHING

The concept of *yinyang* (see page 39) has become inextricably linked to the I-Ching. In almost all translations of the I-Ching a solid line is called a *yang* line while a broken line is called a *yin* line. However, it must be stressed that the ideogram for *yang* (陽) does not appear at all in the original version of the I-Ching while the ideogram for *yin* (陰) appears only once, within the teachings on hexagram 61.

The idea of *yinyang* is probably even older than the I-Ching and the two traditions evolved separately to begin with. However, as the I-Ching became more complex the idea of *yinyang* started to be associated with it. The main writing to introduce the concept of *yinyang* to the I-Ching was the Great Treatise (Dazhuan) dating from the 3rd century BC. The associating of *yin* with female and *yang* with male probably did not reach the I-Ching until Wang Bi's commentaries of the 3rd century AD.

## QUESTIONS OF GENDER

The female and male associations of *yin* and *yang* lines have led some modern commentators to reassess the I-Ching through the lens of gender politics. The simple fact is that the I-Ching was born out of prehistorical traditions and the distribution of roles between genders at that time is unknown. It is thought that the spirit-talkers were female, but that is not known for certain. The introduction of gender-specific elements in the I-Ching did not happen until the Confucian period, when strict social systems were established and women took on a subservient role in many areas. These ideas do not necessarily match up with the original intention behind the I-Ching and are not intrinsic parts of the tradition. What we can be sure of is that the universe does not care whether those who come to it with questions are male or female.

### Yin and yang classifications

Each line position within a hexagram is categorized as either *yin* or *yang* regardless of whether the line occupying that position is solid (*yang*) or broken (*yin*). As shown in the illustration below, the line positions alternate between *yin* and *yang* to make three lines of *yin* and three lines of *yang*. Understand that a *yang* line can be in either a *yin* or a *yang* position, as can a *yin* line – making four possibilities.

In some of the deeper reading methods you can investigate the positive and negative aspects of each of these four permutations. This task is complicated by the fact that there are two versions of the positioning, both of which are shown in the illustration. The first version (on the left) follows the general *yinyang* convention of odd numbers being *yang* and even numbers being *yin*, while the alternative version (on the right) shows *yang* at the top closer to the heavens (a *yang* aspect) and *yin* at the bottom closer to the earth (a *yin* aspect). The first version is the more common system, so you should focus on that one if you need to. But do not worry too much about these; they are only important if you go much deeper into the I-Ching, as illustrated on the next page.

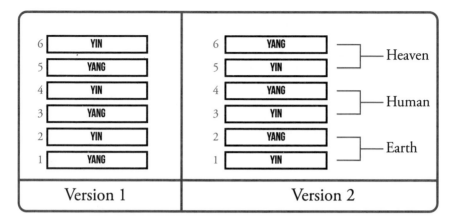

The two systems for attributing *yin* and *yang* to line positions within a hexagram.
The first version is more common.

The illustration below demonstrates how a *yin* line can be in a *yin* position (line 2) or a *yang* position (line 3) and a *yang* line can be in a *yang* position (line 1) or a *yin* position (line 4).

| 6 | YIN | | |
|---|------|------|------|
| 5 | YANG | | |
| 4 | YIN | | *Yang* line in *yin* position |
| 3 | YANG | | *Yin* line in *yang* position |
| 2 | YIN | | *Yin* line in *yin* position |
| 1 | YANG | | *Yang* line in *yang* position |

The four combinations of line type and line position.

When a hexagram or trigram has all *yang* lines, it is *yang*; when it has all *yin* lines, it is *yin*. However, when it comes to a mixture of *yin* and *yang* lines things become more complicated. Contrary to what you might expect, a trigram or hexagram with mainly *yin* lines is actually *yang*, while if it has mainly *yang* lines it is *yin*. The theory is that the minority leads the majority like a captain leading their troops. But, again, this is not so important in a basic casting, and there are variations.

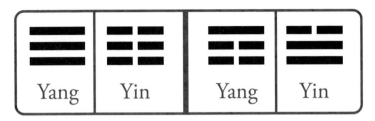

Yinyang classifications of a selection of trigrams.

### Basic *yin* and *yang* numbers

In the *yinyang* system odd numbers are *yang* and even numbers are *yin*. As you will see in the following section, this has a particular bearing on the I-Ching.

Odd numbers are *yang* and even numbers are *yin*.

| | |
|---|---|
| 1 | Yang |
| 2 | Yin |
| 3 | Yang |
| 4 | Yin |
| 5 | Yang |
| 6 | Yin |
| 7 | Yang |
| 8 | Yin |
| 9 | Yang |
| 10 | Yin |

# CASTING A HEXAGRAM

According to the I-Ching the universe delivers its message to you in the form of a hexagram, which you build line by line following one of a number of different casting methods generally based on tossing coins or sorting sticks. Casting with coins is quicker and easier; casting with stalks takes longer and is more complex, but is also older and may give you a greater appreciation of the symbolism of the I-Ching. In this section you will learn about the aspects of the casting process that are common to all methods before being taken through the different methods in detail.

### PREPARING FOR A TRADITIONAL CASTING

Whichever method you choose, if you would like to take a traditional approach to your casting follow these Chinese customs:

- Keep your coins or stalks and your copy of the I-Ching wrapped in rose silk in a box on an altar or other position of honour.

- Do not eat meat or drink alcohol on the day of a casting.

- Take a shower, have a bath or, as a minimum, wash your hands before you start.

- Place a small table in the centre of the room where you are performing the casting.

- Identify the directions of north and south in the room. South is the direction of the spirits and is always the senior direction in Chinese custom. You should sit on the northern side of the table but face south because this places you in a position of submission to your illustrious ancestors.

- Light three incense sticks held in a small container.

- Give a small prayer to the ancestors as you take your equipment from its box and unwrap it.

- Take some time to meditate on your question and then perform your I-Ching casting.

- After it is all over, thank the ancestors and put your I-Ching and paraphernalia away.

Taking steps like these will not in itself give you a "better" answer, but it can be a way of demonstrating your respect for the I-Ching. That is not to say that you cannot respectfully cast a hexagram while away from home. Remember that Confucius was said to carry a copy of the I-Ching with him at all times and use it while he was travelling.

## ASKING YOUR QUESTION

In order to give meaning to an I-Ching casting you first need to formulate a question. Questions should be requests for advice on any future actions you are considering. This can involve interactions with other people, but it should centre around yourself. If other people are in need of advice you can help them make a casting, but *do not* cast for them; the universe communicates with people directly.

There are no rules as to which questions you can and cannot ask. Just try to avoid closed questions (those that give a yes or no answer), as these tend to limit your options when what you are aiming to do is open yourself up to new perspectives. You are specifically asking the universe for an insight that will help guide you through any upcoming issues in your life. Think of it as like asking a wise old friend or relative for the best advice.

The following are examples of potentially productive question types:

- Where will this path take me?

- Which path should I take?

- What should I do if...?

- How do I deal with...?

- What can I do to help...?

- How would doing this affect…?

- What do I need to know?

There are no hard and fast rules as to how you should pose your question – whether, for example, you should hold it silently in your mind or say it out loud – but writing it down on paper is a good way to focus your mind on exactly what you want to ask.

## THE CASTING PROCESS

### Generating the numbers

The process of casting a hexagram involves generating the number 6, 7, 8 or 9 six times, once for each line of the hexagram. Each of those four numbers represents one of the four types of line, as listed below.

| 6 | Transforming *yin* | |
|---|---|---|
| 7 | Static *yang* | |
| 8 | Static *yin* | |
| 9 | Transforming *yang* | |

The transforming (or old) lines are marked in red and the static (or young) lines are in black. Note that the two odd numbers represent *yin* lines and the two even numbers represent *yin* lines (see page 59).

The different casting methods have different ways of generating the numbers 6, 7, 8 and 9, but the result is the same: a hexagram consisting of six lines, each of which is one of the four types of line to be found in the I-Ching.

Note that in some manuals you will see a *yin* line referred to as a "six line" and a *yang* line referred to as a "nine line" regardless of whether it is static or transforming. This terminology refers back to an earlier time when there was no distinction between static and transforming lines and 6 and 9 were the only numbers that could be generated.

## Building from the bottom up

Just as you would when building a house, start your hexagram at the bottom and work your way up to the top. Think of your first line as the foundations of the house, the next four lines as layers of bricks and the final line at the top as the roof.

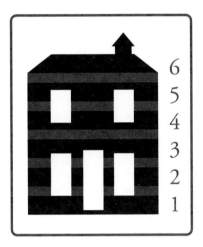

Always start your hexagram at the bottom and work your way up to the top.

The diagram below shows the line-by-line building of hexagram 1 (see the chart on page 10), which is made up entirely of solid lines.

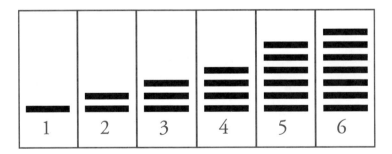

## Writing out your hexagram

Make sure you have a piece of paper and a black pen and a red pen to hand. The black pen is for writing static lines and the red pen is for writing transforming lines. Write out each line as soon as you have generated it – and remember to start at the bottom.

Leave space next to your original hexagram in case you need to create a transformed hexagram (if your original hexagram has any transforming lines). The transformed hexagram does not need any additional casting. You just replicate any static lines from your original hexagram and convert any transforming lines into their opposite (solid to broken; broken to solid). Write all the lines in your transformed hexagram in black – all of these lines have now settled into their final, transformed state.

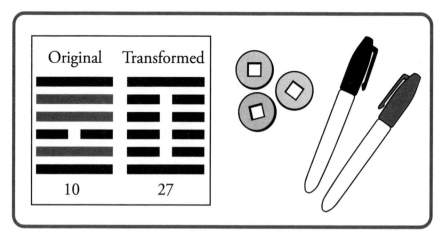

The equipment you will need for a three-coin casting.

## Finding your hexagram

The final stage before going on to find out what your reading might mean in Part 2 is looking up your original hexagram (and the transformed hexagram if there is one) in the chart on page 10.

**Now that you understand the principles of an I-Ching casting, we will move on to explain the individual casting methods.**

### CASTING WITH COINS

Tossing a coin or coins is not the oldest way of casting for the I-Ching, but it has been around for at least a thousand years. It is also the most popular method. Originally, Chinese coins were only inscribed on one side, which made it very easy to distinguish between *yang* (inscribed side) and *yin* (blank side). Now we use heads (*yang*) and tails (*yin*) and this will work for coins from any culture; there is no need to use Chinese coins.

The most common coin-casting method uses three coins. These should be of the same type and shape and have two distinct sides.

---

## HEAVEN AND EARTH

The square hole in a Chinese coin represents the hard angles of earth (*yin*), while the roundness of the coin itself represents the heavens above (*yang*).

---

The process you are about to undertake is very simple. All you need to do is throw the three coins all at the same time. Coins landing heads up are allotted a value of 3 and those landing tails up have a value of 2. The table below shows the four possible outcomes of a three-coin toss and the total value for each outcome, which ranges from 6 to 9. Use the table to convert your coin toss into a line of your hexagram and draw the line on your piece of paper (remembering to start from the bottom line and use a black pen for static lines and a red pen for transforming lines). You will do this six times to create your hexagram.

| Result | Calculation | Number | Line type |
|---|---|---|---|
| Tails x 3 | 2 + 2 + 2 | 6 | Transforming *yin* line |
| Tails x 2, Heads x 1 | 2 + 2 + 3 | 7 | Static *yang* line |
| Heads x 2, Tails x 1 | 3 + 3 + 2 | 8 | Static *yin* line |
| Heads x 3 | 3 + 3 + 3 | 9 | Transforming *yang* line |

For absolute clarity, the following images will show the connections between the coins you throw and the type of line you need to draw.

If you get three tails, draw a transforming *yin* line in red.
This is also known as a "six line".

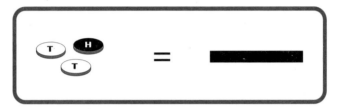

If you get two tails and one head, draw a static *yang* line in black.
This is also known as a "seven line".

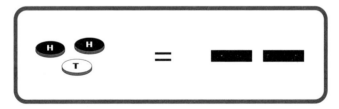

If you get two heads and one tail, draw a static *yin* line in black.
This is also known as an "eight line".

If you get three heads, draw a transforming *yang* line in red.
This is also known as a "nine line".

## Example coin cast

The diagram below shows an example breakdown of six coin tosses that would produce hexagram 17.

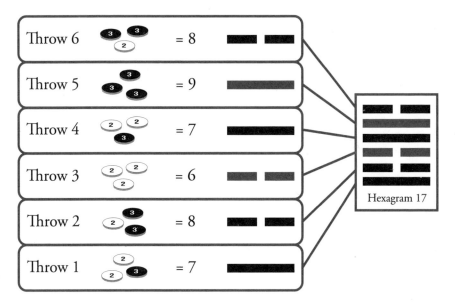

As you will have noticed, the third and fifth lines of the example hexagram above are transforming. The next diagram shows the process of creating the second or transformed hexagram by converting the two red lines to their black opposite.

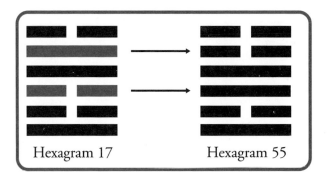

Hexagram 17          Hexagram 55

Once you have found your hexagram in the chart on page 10, turn to the entry for that hexagram in Part 2 and read the title, the **Read me first** section and the individual line commentaries for any transforming lines (*do not* look at the line commentaries for the static lines). Then turn to the entry for the transformed hexagram (if there is one), but only look at the title and the **Read me first** section for that hexagram. That takes you to the end of your core reading. To see how to go further into a reading, turn to page 96.

---

## DIFFERENT SYSTEMS, SAME MESSAGE

The method given here is the most common, but do not worry if you see other versions. For example, in Margaret Pearson's edition of the I-Ching heads have a value of 2 and tails 3; Alfred Huang's system is different again. These variations could call into question the entire I-Ching. However, being outside of time and space, the universe is always ahead of you. It will know which system you are using and adjust accordingly to deliver the message you need.

---

### The one-coin method

The following alternative method requires only a single coin. It can be used if you need a quick and simple answer, but the traditional three-coin and stalk methods are preferable.

Toss a coin six times and roll a die once to quickly get an answer from the universe.

Toss a coin six times to build a hexagram. If it is heads, record a solid *yang* line; and if it is tails, record a broken *yin* line. Remember to build your hexagram from the bottom up. After six coin throws you will have your hexagram.

Done this way you will get no transforming lines, so it will be a very simple reading. However, you can add depth by rolling a die to determine one transforming line (and, therefore, produce a transforming hexagram). If you roll a 1, the bottom line of your hexagram will be transforming, and so on. The odds are different from the more traditional methods but you are not trying to play the maths, you are asking the universe for help.

## CASTING WITH STALKS

Around 3,000 years ago, the ancient Chinese began to turn from divination by burning animal bones toward a new method involving the sorting of stalks from the yarrow or milfoil plant (*Achillea millefolium*). It is believed that originally the sticks used were very long and, according to some accounts, different social classes had different length sticks: 9 feet long for an emperor; 7 feet for lesser royalty; 5 feet for high officials; and 3 feet for gentlemen. Divination with bones and, later, sticks was a tribal ritual (coins, in contrast, were better suited to private readings). Imagine a stage holding people moving around with long poles as a full-blown public divination proceeded and the other members of the clan watched on, waiting for the results. In truth, it is not known for certain what form such events would have taken, but it is believed that stalk-sorting rituals were originally communal in nature and reduced in scale over time from the tribal to the royal to the individual.

The following system, which is the one used by most people today, comes from the Dazhuan, the first of the Ten Wings (see page 28). It dates from around 500 BC, roughly 500 years after King Wen created the basic outline for the I-Ching.

Casting with stalks is simple enough to do, but quite hard to explain. Over the next few pages you will find every stage in the process laid out and illustrated to make it as easy as possible to follow, but it may also be helpful to watch a demonstration online from a reputable source. In the diagrams below, the red stalks represent the ones you are working with in that stage while the ones from the previous stage are shown in grey. To generate each line of your hexagram you have to repeat a set process of dividing stalks three times. This means that you will divide your stalks a total of 18 times in order to build a complete hexagram. You may not master the system immediately, but if you take your time and follow the instructions carefully you will soon get there.

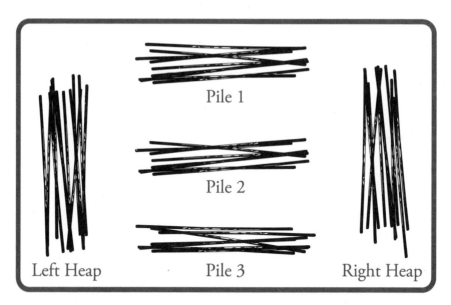

Pile 1

Pile 2

Left Heap · Pile 3 Right Heap

Keep your divination space neat. Ensure there is room for a heap of stalks to the left and a heap to the right with space in the middle to lay out three horizontal piles in front of you. For clarity, we will use the word "heap" for the collections of stalks to the left and right and "pile" for the ones in the middle.

## Sorting the stalks

The process described below is the one used by Professor Richard Ho of the Sinological Development Charitable Foundation. At time of publication, his demonstration can be viewed online. You may find variations in other books or online. For example, some sources may tell you to remove the first stalks from the opposite side. And if you are left-handed, you might find it easier to place the stalks between the fingers of your right hand. It does not really matter in which order you deal with the two heaps or which hand you use. The most important thing is that you do the counting correctly.

## Step 1

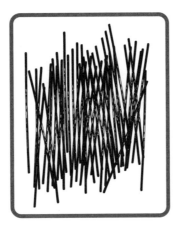

Take 50 stalks and put them together in one heap. You do not need to invest in an expensive I-Ching set containing yarrow stalks; cheap wooden barbecue skewers would work just as well. For this system to work you must have exactly 50 stalks to begin with.

## Step 2

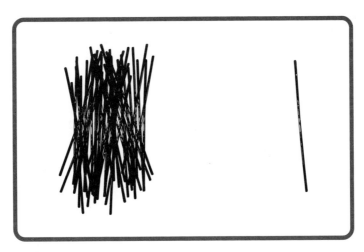

Take one stalk away from the pile of 50 and discard it to leave you with 49 stalks. You do not have to touch this single stalk again until you cast the next line of your hexagram. You should not use this stalk again until you return all the way back to step 1.

## Step 3

Separate the 49 stalks into two random heaps. You will need space to place one heap on your right and one heap on your left.

## Step 4

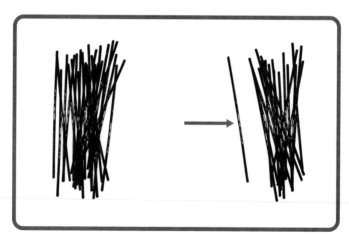

Take one stalk from the heap on the **right**.

Step 5

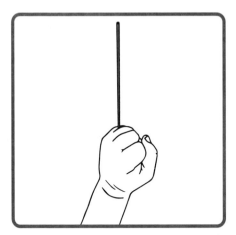

Place the stalk you have picked out between the little finger and ring finger of your **left** hand.

Step 6

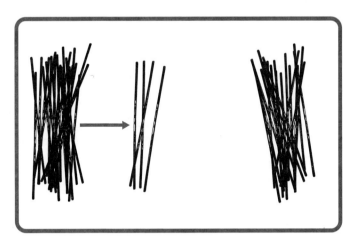

Take away stalks from the **left** heap, four stalks at a time, until you have between one and four stalks remaining in the heap. If you do not have one, two, three or four stalks left, something has gone wrong.

Step 7

Place the remaining one, two, three or four stalks from the left heap between the ring finger and middle finger of the **left** hand.

Step 8

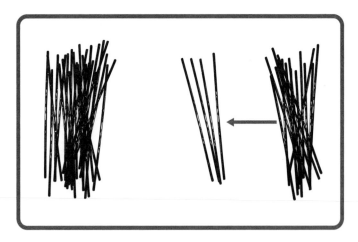

Take away stalks from the **right** heap, four stalks at a time, until you have between one and four stalks remaining in the heap. Again, if you do not have one, two, three or four stalks left, something has gone wrong.

Step 9

Place the remaining one, two, three or four stalks from the right heap between the middle finger and index finger of the **left** hand.

**At this point there will be either five or nine stalks between the fingers of your left hand. If there is any other number of stalks, you have made a mistake and you will need to start again.**

Step 10

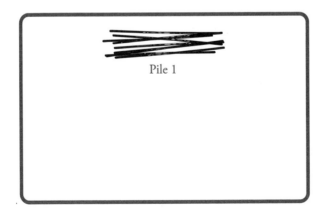

Pile 1

Take the stalks that are between your fingers and place them horizontally in front of you in a horizontal position. This will become pile 1. Leave space for pile 2 and pile 3.

Put all the stalks apart from those that are in pile 1 back into a single heap ready to start the next round. Do not add the original one taken away in step 2. That remains out of the pile until you return to step 1.

Step 11

Separate the stalks into two random heaps – leaving pile 1 in its place – and position one heap to the left and one heap to the right.

Step 12

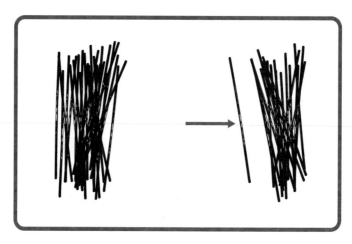

Take one stalk from the heap on the **right**.

Step 13

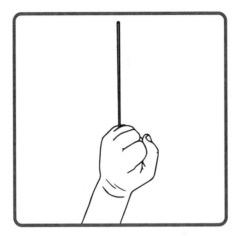

Place the stalk you have picked out between the little finger and ring finger of your **left** hand.

Step 14

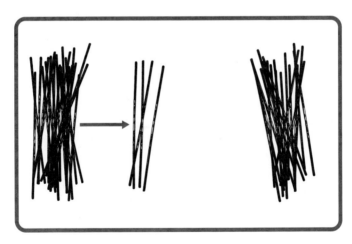

Take away stalks from the **left** heap, four stalks at a time, until you have between one and four stalks remaining in the heap. If you do not have one, two, three or four stalks left, something has gone wrong.

Step 15

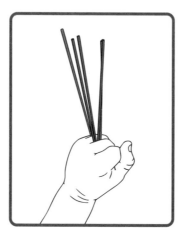

Place the remaining one, two, three or four stalks from the left heap between the ring finger and middle finger of the **left** hand.

Step 16

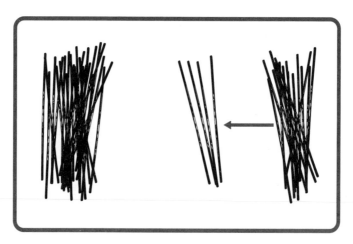

Take away stalks from the **right** heap, four stalks at a time, until you have between one and four stalks remaining in the heap. Again, if you do not have one, two, three or four stalks left, something has gone wrong.

Step 17

Place the remaining one, two, three or four stalks from the right heap between the middle finger and index finger of the **left** hand.

**At this point there will be either four or eight stalks between the fingers of your left hand (*not* five or nine, as was the case last time). If there is any other number of stalks, you have made a mistake and you will need to start again.**

Step 18

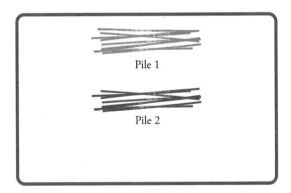

Pile 1

Pile 2

Take the stalks that are between your fingers and place them horizontally in front of you in a horizontal position below pile 1 to form pile 2. You now have two piles as shown in the image above. Leave space for pile 3.

**Put all the stalks apart from those that are in pile 1 and pile 2 back into a single heap ready to start the next round.**

Step 19

Separate the stalks into two random heaps – leaving pile 1 and pile 2 in their place – and position one heap to the left and one heap to the right.

Step 20

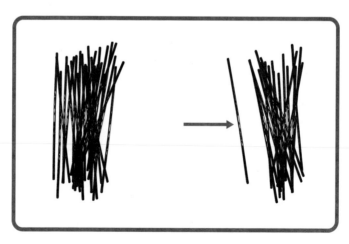

Take one stalk from the heap on the **right**.

Step 21

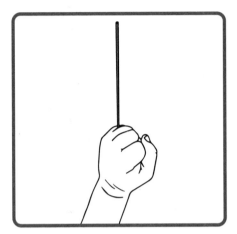

Place the stalk you have picked out between the little finger and ring finger of your **left** hand.

Step 22

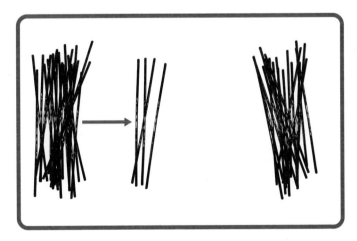

Take away stalks from the **left** heap, four stalks at a time, until you have between one and four stalks remaining in the heap. If you do not have one, two, three or four stalks left, something has gone wrong.

Step 23

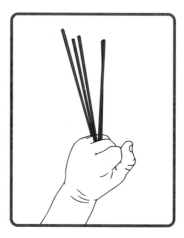

Place the remaining one, two, three or four stalks from the left heap between the ring finger and middle finger of the **left** hand.

Step 24

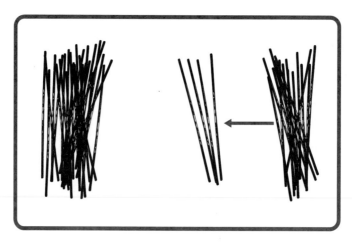

Take away stalks from the **right** heap, four stalks at a time, until you have between one and four stalks remaining in the heap. Again, if you do not have one, two, three or four stalks left, something has gone wrong.

Step 25

Place the remaining one, two, three or four stalks from the right heap between the middle finger and index finger of the **left** hand.

**At this point there will be either four or eight stalks between the fingers of your left hand. If there is any other number of stalks, you have made a mistake and you will need to start again.**

Step 26

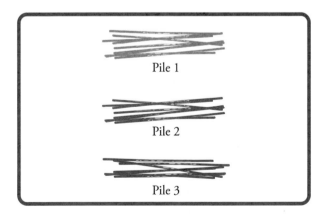

Pile 1

Pile 2

Pile 3

Take the stalks that are between your fingers and place them horizontally in front of you in a horizontal position below pile 2 to form pile 3. You now have three piles as shown in the image above.

**This marks the end of the first run of six. The next step is to convert these three piles into the first line of your hexagram.**

## Converting your piles into values

You will now have three piles in front of you, with the following number of stalks in each pile:

- Pile 1: either 5 or 9 stalks

- Pile 2: either 4 or 8 stalks

- Pile 3: either 4 or 8 stalks

You now have to assign a value of either 2 or 3 to each of these piles depending on the number of stalks they contain (just as you do for each coin in a three-coin toss). The image below shows how to find the value of each of your piles.

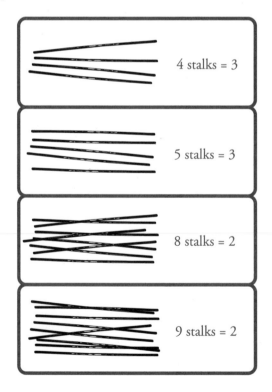

Next, add together the values of each of your three piles to get an overall value. Just as in coin casting, this will be 6, 7, 8 or 9. Each of these overall values corresponds to one of the four types of I-Ching line, as listed below. This tells you what kind of line to record for the first line of your hexagram (and subsequent lines when you do the remaining five runs).

| 6 | Transforming *yin* | |
|---|---|---|
| 7 | Static *yang* | |
| 8 | Static *yin* | |
| 9 | Transforming *yang* | |

Use this image to convert your overall value into a line type. Remember to build your hexagram from the bottom up.

The following two examples show exactly how to turn your three piles of stalks into a single line of your hexagram.

| 9 stalks | = | 2 |
|---|---|---|
| 8 stalks | = | 2 |
| 4 stalks | = | 3 |

$$2+2+3=7$$ Static *yang*

This casting has produced an overall value of 7, which creates a static *yang* line to be written in black.

| 5 stalks | = | 3 |
|---|---|---|
| 4 stalks | = | 3 |
| 4 stalks | = | 3 |

$$3+3+3=9$$ Transforming *yang*

This casting has produced an overall value of 9, which creates a transforming *yang* line to be written in red.

HOW TO USE THE I-CHING

**Repeat the process to generate all six lines**

Having been through this whole process, you only have one line of your hexagram to show for it. So, now you need to put all 50 stalks back in a single heap and repeat the process from the beginning another five times. After six full rounds of dividing stalks, making piles, assigning values and converting to line types you will have built a full hexagram. As with other casting methods, convert any transforming lines to their opposites in order to create the transformed hexagram, look up the hexagram or hexagrams in the chart on page 10 and turn to the readings in Part 2.

---

## RAPID STALK CASTING

In temples across east Asia you may find a highly simplified version of stalk divination. It uses a box containing 64 sticks numbered from 1 to 64. The idea is to shake the box until one of the sticks protrudes out of a small hole. The number on the stick corresponds to the number of your hexagram. This is a quick way to get a basic reading.

---

### CASTING WITH EIGHT TOKENS

There is another casting method which requires eight tokens and a six-sided die. This is a quick way to do many readings if you are working in a group. The idea is that each of the tokens represents one of the eight trigrams. You could use, for example, coins of the same denomination but different years of minting, different-coloured gemstones of the same form, or cards or similar-sized pebbles each with a different trigram drawn on it.

Follow these principles when sourcing your tokens:

- The tokens must feel the same, but be visually distinct from each other.

- They must all fit into a bag.

- If you are representing the trigrams on your tokens, you must indicate which way to read them – for example, by marking a dot at the top of each trigram or snipping off the top corner of each card.

- If your tokens do not visually represent the trigrams, you need to assign a different trigram to each object and write them out in a list so that you can remember which is which.

The casting process is as follows:

1 Place all the tokens in a bag and mix them up.

2 Reach in and pull out a token at random. On a piece of paper write out the trigram that the selected token represents. Be sure to keep the lines in the correct order. This is your lower trigram and it goes at the bottom of your hexagram.

3 Put the token back in the bag before you pick the upper trigram. This is essential because you must be able to pick from all eight trigrams *both* times.

4 Reach in and pull out a token for a second time. Carefully write out the trigram that this token represents above the first trigram. This is your upper trigram. Now you have your complete hexagram.

5 Next, identify which is the transforming line by rolling the die once. Rolling a 1 means that the bottom line is the transforming line, and so on.

6 Draw the transformed hexagram next to the original hexagram, identify the two hexagrams using the chart on page 10 and go to your readings.

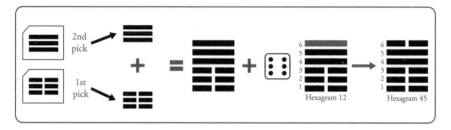

In this example, the user has picked the two trigrams comprising hexagram 12, then rolled a 6 to make the top line transforming. This means that the transformed hexagram is hexagram 45.

# READING YOUR CASTING

Having cast your hexagram, you now need to decipher the message that it contains.

### FINDING YOUR HEXAGRAM

To be able to access the reading attached to your hexagram you will first need to identify your hexagram using the chart on page 10. For ease of reference, the chart organizes the hexagrams according to their upper and lower trigram.

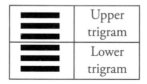

A hexagram is constructed of two trigrams: the upper trigram at the top and the lower trigram at the bottom.

Each column of the chart contains hexagrams with the same upper trigram along the top and also each row down the side has hexagrams with the same lower trigram. All you have to do is match them up. Therefore, to find your hexagram look at the top of the table and find the three lines which match the top of your hexagram and then look down the left side of the table and find the three lines which match the bottom of your hexagram. Then follow the column down and the row across to the point where they meet (see illustration below). This is how to find the number of your hexagram.

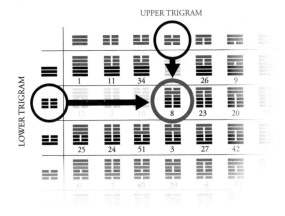

Look down the column containing the upper trigram and across the row
containing the lower trigram to find the number of your hexagram.

The hexagram readings in Part 2 of this book are arranged in numerical order, so it will be easy to find the section devoted to your hexagram either by referring to the Contents or simply by flicking through the pages.

### ORIGINAL AND TRANSFORMED HEXAGRAMS

As you will have realized by now, more often than not you will cast at least one transforming line in your hexagram. By converting any transforming lines in your original hexagram to their opposite, you will receive a second part to your reading in the form of a second, transformed hexagram.

The first part of the reading, from the original hexagram, relates to your immediate situation. It gives an outline of the circumstances you are in or the things you have to deal with right now. The second part of the reading, from the transformed hexagram, is concerned with your future, particularly the changes you will have to make or go through to get the most positive result. You can understand this as the universe giving you the tools you need to steer through a situation that is puzzling you, so that you can get from one point in your life to the next.

If you do not receive any transforming lines in your casting, it means that the answer is simple enough to be contained entirely within one hexagram.

Some researchers believe that ancient users of the I-Ching always converted every line of the original hexagram into a second, fully transformed hexagram, but this system is now only used by a few.

The process of converting the original hexagram into a transformed hexagram is explained in the section on casting with coins (see page 64). See below for a reminder.

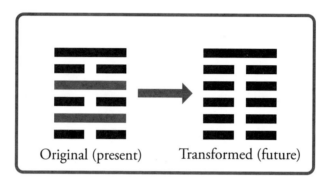

Original (present)    Transformed (future)

Transforming solid lines turn into static broken lines, and transforming broken lines turn into static solid lines. Lines can transform only once, so all red (transforming) lines in the original hexagram become black (static) in the transformed hexagram.

This is the standard transformation process, but there are also various alternative systems (see page 93).

**An I-Ching reading generally comes in two parts. The first hexagram is about your present state; the second, transformed hexagram shows you the way forward. If you only get one hexagram, that is your full answer.**

HOW TO READ YOUR CASTING

If you look at the readings in Part 2 of this book, you will see that for each hexagram there is a title, an opening statement entitled **Read me first** and individual commentaries for each line (to be read only for any transforming lines in your original hexagram). To get the most out of your reading, always follow the process laid out below.

### Step 1 – read the title
First there is the title of the hexagram to consider. Take time to reflect on what it means for you and your situation before you go any further. This will establish the way in which you approach the whole reading. Bear in mind that different translations carry different connotations. An unreliable translation can bend your whole reading out of shape. The hexagram titles used in this book are based on a range of sources so that they do not lean too heavily on any single interpretation.

### Step 2 – read the opening statement
The next step is to understand the meaning of the hexagram as a whole and how it relates to you. In this book this is called the **Read me first** section. This will offer you an overview of the situation and give you hints as to how you should act. If you have cast no transforming lines, your reading will be complete at this point.

### Step 3 – read the teachings for any transforming lines
If you have cast any transforming lines in your original hexagram, read the individual commentaries for those specific lines. *Do not* read the commentaries for static lines in your hexagram. Normally, you would read the teachings for all transforming lines, but if you have a lot of transforming lines the teachings can contradict each other. Therefore, some commentators recommend narrowing your focus (see box overleaf).

### Step 4 – read the transformed hexagram
For the transformed hexagram (see page 64), if you have one, read only the title and the **Read me first** section. Think of these in terms of your future and the effect any actions you are considering will have. That will complete your reading.

### Relationships between trigrams
Also look at each of the two trigrams that make up your hexagram; their relationship to each other will help develop an overall picture of the situation. This is one of the oldest ways to understand the I-Ching. In Part 2 of this book the opening statement for each hexagram gives a brief explanation of the significance of the trigram relationship in that hexagram.

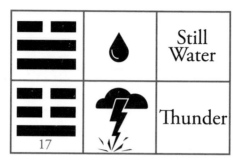

| | | |
|---|---|---|
| ▬▬ ▬▬ | 💧 | Still Water |
| ▬▬ ▬▬ 17 | ⛈ | Thunder |

To Follow

Hexagram 17 has the **Still Water** trigram above the **Thunder** trigram. Thunder will cause ripples in still water and those ripples follow each other. Therefore, the overall meaning of this hexagram is "following and accompanying".

## MULTIPLE TRANSFORMING LINES

If you get more than one transforming line in your casting, normally you would read the line commentary for each of them. However, the more transforming lines there are, the more likely it is that you will receive mixed messages from the individual line commentaries. The researcher Alfred Huang has given the following set of instructions to help you home in on the most significant line in your casting:

- If you have one transforming line, focus on that one.

- If you get two opposite transforming lines in your original hexagram, one line being a transforming *yin* line and the other being a transforming *yang* line, focus on the commentary for the *yin* one (the broken line).

- If you have two transforming lines of the same type (either both *yang* or both *yin*), focus on the commentary for the one that is closer to the bottom of the hexagram.

- If there are three transforming lines of either type, focus on the commentary for the one in the middle position.

- If there are four transforming lines of either type, do not focus on any of them. Instead, focus on the commentary for the *static* line that is closer to the top of the hexagram.

- If there are five transforming lines of either type, focus on the commentary for the only static line.

- If all six lines are transforming then the transformed hexagram will be far more important to your situation than the original hexagram. Make sure to study the transformed hexagram in more depth and put more emphasis on it than the original hexagram.

You do not have to follow this system. You may prefer to follow the standard procedure of reading the commentaries for all the transforming lines you have cast.

ALTERNATIVE READING METHODS

As we have seen, in a standard reading of the I-Ching any transforming lines in the original hexagram are converted into their opposites to form a second, transformed hexagram. However, over the centuries different methods were used to extract divine messages from the I-Ching. You do not have to use any of these ways if you prefer to follow the standard reading system (see page 88), but they are explained here for those who wish to approach the I-Ching from a different angle.

## The direct opposite hexagram

To produce the direct opposite hexagram simply transform every line of the original hexagram into its opposite. When casting your hexagram, the distinction between transforming and static lines is no longer relevant; all you need to record is whether each line is solid or broken. Your reading then consists of the title and opening statement for the original hexagram and the transformed hexagram. The individual line commentaries are not read. This is believed to have been the ancient way.

Following this system means that a certain hexagram will always transform into the same hexagram each time, which limits the variations in message you can receive. In contrast, the standard system allows a hexagram to transform into any one of the other 63.

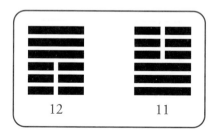

Using the direct opposite hexagram system, hexagram 12 will always transform into hexagram 11 and vice versa.

## The hidden hexagram

It is believed by some that inside any hexagram there is a hidden hexagram which tells you what is at the core of your question. The hidden hexagram has a lower trigram comprising the second, third and fourth lines of your original hexagram, and an upper trigram comprising the third, fourth and fifth lines of the original hexagram (see illustration below). As with the direct opposite hexagram, there is only one possible hidden hexagram for each hexagram.

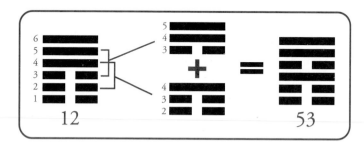

Created from the middle four lines of a hexagram, the hidden hexagram is believed to point toward the deeper cause or issue related to your question. As this example shows, hexagram 53 is the hexagram hidden within hexagram 12.

## The steps of change

If you have cast more than one transforming line, you can gain a more detailed reading by building a new hexagram for each individual transforming line. You will end up with: your original hexagram, your final, fully transformed hexagram (with all transforming lines converted to their opposite, as normal) and between two and six partially transformed hexagrams (each with just one of the transforming lines in your original casting converted to its opposite). Do this by working from the bottom up (see the example illustrated below).

You should read the hexagrams in the following way:

- Your original hexagram represents the current situation.

- The partially transformed hexagrams show the process of change you need to go through.

- The final transformed hexagram shows you the way forward for the future.

The partially transformed hexagrams in your reading do not necessarily lay out a linear progression. See them all, however many there are, as a combined solution to the problem, all working together to show you the change you need.

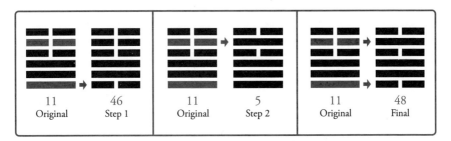

|   11   |  46   |   11   |   5    |   11   |  48   |
|:------:|:-----:|:------:|:------:|:------:|:-----:|
|Original|Step 1 |Original|Step 2 |Original|Final  |

In this example, the two transforming lines in the original hexagram each convert individually to create two separate transformed hexagrams and then convert together to create a final, fully transformed hexagram.

## GOING DEEPER INTO THE I-CHING

The I-Ching can be engaged with in a variety of ways: as a divination tool, as a moral compass, as a window into Chinese thought and understanding, as a key with which to unlock prehistory, and so on. Whether you want to experiment with different processes and consult a variety of translations and commentaries, or whether you prefer to keep it simple by sticking to the standard casting and reading methods and the mainstream interpretations, is totally up to you. Either approach can be beneficial. Perhaps start with the readings in this book and then, like any good student of the I-Ching, investigate the various other versions available which go into greater depth. Always remember that the I-Ching is unchanging; different translations and interpretations only make it *appear* to change.

### Comparing translations

There are many different I-Ching editions and if you compare what they have to say about the different hexagrams you will soon find that they vary considerably. This is to be expected, given the vagueness of the original I-Ching. But which source to believe? If you rely solely on a literal translation of the original text, you may find it so open-ended and the interpretations so arbitrary that you cannot reach any conclusion. On the other hand, it might allow you to keep an open mind and make you more receptive to the message that the universe is sending. But, there again, it might also lead you to interpret a message in your own favour. Newer, more user-friendly editions are easier to understand but they may accidentally misinterpret the original to fit a modern worldview, which may lead you to the wrong conclusions. This is not a new problem; even the ancient Chinese commentators disagreed over the original meanings of the I-Ching. This book has attempted to overcome this problem by providing interpretations based on a range of different sources.

### See the I-Ching through your own eyes

If you dig too deep into the commentaries, both ancient and modern, there is a danger that you will miss the main point of the message, which may be staring right at you. Remember that the original I-Ching masters did not need anyone else's interpretations nor did they even exist at that time. Today there is a move by some to return to a more self-sufficient approach to the I-Ching.

## THE MATHEMATICS OF CHANCE

Some scholars have taken a mathematical approach to the I-Ching, calculating the probability of all manner of outcomes. For example, using the three-coin casting method:

- With each three-coin toss, there is a 25% chance of drawing a transforming line.

- There is an 18% chance of casting a hexagram that has no transforming lines.

- There is a 0.02% chance of casting a hexagram that has nothing but transforming lines.

These statistics are interesting, particularly to those who seek to rationalize the workings of the I-Ching, but if you come at the I-Ching with logic and rationality you will miss the whole point of it. If you truly believe in the power of the I-Ching, the odds do not matter: nothing can change what the universe intends for you. You will receive the correct answer, even if you do not understand it, like it or want it.

We cannot know how the I-Ching was read in ancient times. The process may have been simpler than that used today, or more complex. The depth in which you study the I-Ching is up to you. However, do not lose sight of what you are using it for: to find your message.

# ACTING ON THE I-CHING

With your casting and reading complete, it is time to sit back and allow the message to sink in. Take time to reflect on its meaning before converting the message into action.

### UNDERSTANDING THE MESSAGE FROM THE DAO

The great paradox of the I-Ching is that it can be the most reliable guide or the most treacherous saboteur, depending on how you interpret what it is telling you. Be careful not to let your own ideas distort the message. Do not overlook the obvious point, and recheck both the original text and the commentators to make sure that you have not gone off track.

You will see in Part 2 of this book that certain messages recur throughout the I-Ching. Examples include:

- This is a good situation.

- This is a bad situation.

- Go forward now.

- Do not go forward now.

- Seek help.

- Do it alone.

- Maintain virtue for success.

- There is someone evil near you.

- There is a teacher you have to find.

- Heaven protects you.

- You are not in favour with heaven.

When you receive a message like that in your reading, take heed of it. Over-analysis can lead you to lose sight of the core learning.

**Keep your head grounded in reality. Do not see what you want to see. Check and recheck to make sure you understand what the universe is telling you.**

### WHEN TO PERFORM A DIVINATION AGAIN

Having just finished a reading, some people ask when they can cast again. The answer is anytime you like, but it must be for the right reasons. If you have a succession of serious questions that come from an honest heart then ask them, but casting for casting's sake is a misuse of your channel to the universe. If you had a direct line to your boss, they would get annoyed if you kept calling them for the slightest of questions. Think for yourself first. Always be respectful in your approach to the I-Ching and be honest with yourself about the validity of a question. Never cast the same question more than once in quick succession just to get a different result from the one you got first time.

**Never question the answer the universe has given you and never ask for a different result. The universe has told you what you need. It is your task to dig deep and apply it.**

### USING THE I-CHING TO ENRICH YOUR LIFE WITH DECISIONS

The I-Ching can be like a compass to help you navigate the uncharted waters of the future. Engage with it to help you make better decisions, but also to help yourself develop into a person who naturally seeks a better future for all. However, do not rely too heavily on the I-Ching. Remember that you are one of the most advanced beings in the known universe and, as such, you have the spiritual capacity to do good things in the world without needing divine advice. But if you are truly stuck, ask the universe for help.

# CHANGE MAINTAINED: A CONCLUSION

Throughout its long history the I-Ching has influenced countless people across the world and it continues to do so. What has been presented here is the most common way of using the I-Ching accompanied by a glimpse at various other traditions. There is a trend to return to the original format without modern interpretation, as in Margaret Pearson's *The Original I-Ching* (Tuttle). However, this is counterbalanced by attempts to take the I-Ching into completely new directions, as in Richard Rudd's *The Gene Keys* (Watkins). Overall, this rich variety of approaches points to the enduring relevance of this intriguing and powerful work.

**At this point you can stop reading and start casting. The rest of the book is devoted to the commentaries for each of the 64 hexagrams and so you will only need to refer to it once you have made a casting. All that is left to be said is that you should enjoy the I-Ching, make it a new aspect of your life and see it as a real communication with the divine, no matter how you interpret that word. Each message is just for you.**

## QUICK-FIRE SUMMARY

Before you get started you may find it helpful to refer to the following, which lays out the I-Ching process in simple steps:

1 Formulate a question to ask the universe.

2 Cast your hexagram, using one of the casting methods provided (see pages 62–88).

3 If you have cast any transforming lines, convert them to their opposite to build a second, transformed hexagram (see pages 89–90).

4 Find your original hexagram and transformed hexagram (if you have one) in the chart on page 10.

5 Turn to the section for your original hexagram in Part 2 of this book. Look at the title of the hexagram and the **Read me first**

section. If you have no transforming lines, you finish here. If you do have transforming lines, move on to the next step.

6   Look at the individual line commentaries for any transforming lines in your original hexagram.

7   Now turn to the section for your transformed hexagram. Look at the title and the **Read me first** section only. This is the end of your reading.

PART
TWO

# THE I-CHING

# HEXAGRAMS

The second part of the book contains the complete explanations of the 64 hexagrams, divided into two sections: the Upper Canon and the Lower Canon. The teachings provided are not direct translations of the original Chinese but an amalgamation of interpretations by many authors. This is done in an attempt to present the generally agreed interpretation while highlighting any variations. Alternative interpretations are accompanied with the commentator's name in brackets so that you can, if you wish, refer to the bibliography and investigate in more detail. Generally, these differing explanations complement each other. However, occasionally they directly contradict each other. In these instances you will need to reach your own conclusion as to which interpretation speaks to your situation.

易經

# THE I-CHING:
# UPPER CANON

# THE I-CHING:
# UPPER CANON

Consisting of the first 30 hexagrams of the I-Ching, the Upper Canon is seen as representing the heavens. It is, therefore, associated with *yang* energy (see page 39). However, it should be remembered that the original I-Ching came before *yinyang* theory had been fully developed. Therefore, when performing a casting and a reading simply go to the hexagram the universe has given you and do not read too much into whether it is part of the Upper Canon or the Lower Canon.

## HEXAGRAM 1

**This hexagram represents: a stage of creation and the power of initiation**

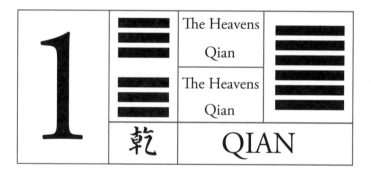

| 1 | The Heavens<br>Qian | |
|---|---|---|
| | The Heavens<br>Qian | |
| | 乾 | QIAN |

**READ ME FIRST**

This hexagram appearing in your casting refers to creative power, success and pushing forward. The lower and upper trigrams are both **The Heavens**. This represents massive creative energy and shows that your situation is founded on true power. This hexagram is associated with dragons, which in Chinese culture represent superior people or people of excellent ability. For you there is great potential ahead if you make the correct decisions.

**If you do not have any transforming lines:** consider whether to wait and seek advice from a trusted person. Avoid being overconfident, no matter what. This is a time of great opportunity so use it wisely.

**If you do have transforming lines:** consult those lines within this hexagram for a more direct answer. Then transform your hexagram and focus just on the **Read me first** section of the new hexagram to discover what you should do.

## Bottom line

If you have this as a transforming line, you should not take immediate action but wait and observe. Be patient. Your time is coming so look out for the opportunity and then seize it. In this situation, it is a time for more or better planning.

## Second line up

If you have this as a transforming line, seek advice from someone you trust. Set your goals (Huang) and let the experience and wisdom of another guide you. In this situation, it is best to see what has worked before.

## Third line up

If you have this as a transforming line, keep your feet on the ground, do not get ahead of yourself, work hard, finalize your plans for success and think greatly on the situation. Avoid being over ambitious and remain centred. Stay on the correct path (Huang). In this situation, do not rush forward.

## Fourth line up

If you have this as a transforming line, it is acceptable to wait and rethink your next move. Go back over your situation and give it a fresh look or even test out your plans with small moves. Stop, observe and find the best timing (Huang). Alternatively, do not take too long before deciding; now is the time (Adcock). In this situation, look at the issue again and find a better approach.

## Fifth line up

If you have this as a transforming line, it is a warning that you should consult a trusted adviser, even though your plans may be going smoothly. It need not be a friend, but it has to be someone you respect for their wisdom and knowledge. Also, if you have people in place below you whom you are relying on to strengthen your cause, make sure they are the right people. If your purpose is apparent to you, then it soon will be

108

time to move forward. Alternatively, join with others and move forward (Adcock). Now is the time to put yourself into action (Huang). In this situation, talk to someone who has been in your position before.

## Top line

If you have this as a transforming line, remember that people are often over-confident and misguided. Those who see no faults in themselves may be reckless. Make sure that you do not fall into the trap of self-congratulation, or excessive belief in your own ability. Act with humility. Do not push beyond the point where you should stop (Huang). In this situation, getting carried away with yourself is a risk.

# HEXAGRAM 2

**This hexagram represents: fertility, creativity, diligence, acceptance and receiving**

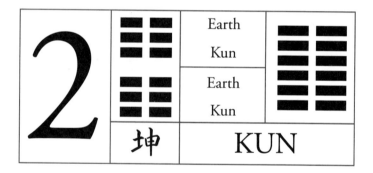

| | | Earth | |
| | | Kun | |
| | | Earth | |
| | | Kun | |
| 2 | | 坤 | KUN |

READ ME FIRST

This hexagram appearing in your casting represents stability and perseverance. The lower and upper trigrams are both **Earth**. The image is of places deep within the earth, implying quietness, nourishing and safety. It is concerned with the moment before action, knowing when to hold your ground, and preparing for movement in the future. You must understand your own ability and not push on before your time; let things grow and mature before taking action.

THE ULTIMATE I-CHING

**If you do not have any transforming lines:** in your situation you should be humble, modest and keep your head down yet remain firm in your own ideas. Take stock of the people around you; distance yourself from those who are a bad influence and turn instead toward comrades who can help. Maintaining a quiet diligence will bring success. Avoid attention from others, control your ego and let nature take its course.

**If you do have transforming lines:** consult those lines within this hexagram for a more direct answer. Then transform your hexagram and focus just on the **Read me first** section of the new hexagram to discover what you should do.

### Bottom line

If you have this as a transforming line, prepare for the future now and think before you act. Store up a portion of your current resources for leaner times ahead and concentrate your inner energy for future events. No matter how much you have now, whether you think it a little or a lot, keep some in reserve. The original Chinese talks about treading on frost to make ice, which means building a stronger foundation for the future. In this situation, being ready far in advance is best.

### Second line up

If you have this as a transforming line, let nature take its course and focus on your talents. Consider helping other people out with their issues or leading by example. Even if you are not highly skilled, simple honesty and hard work will get you there. In this situation, do not force it but do not be idle.

### Third line up

If you have this as a transforming line, be confident in your own abilities but do not boast. Do not let any successes go to your head and know that sometimes you have to support others. Push forward if the goal is in sight (Huang). In this situation, keep quiet and do not push yourself ahead of others.

### Fourth line up

If you have this as a transforming line, avoid looking for praise and do not tell everyone about your successes or failures. Keep a low profile and wait

THE I-CHING: UPPER CANON

for any problems to pass. Alternatively, trust your gut feelings (Adcock) but remain cautious (Huang). In this situation, focus on your own mind and internals.

### Fifth line up

If you have this as a transforming line, maintain discretion and keep your head down. Just keep doing what you are doing and let your efforts speak for themselves. In this situation, let others see you without seeking to be noticed.

### Top line

If you have this as a transforming line, devote yourself to a higher purpose and avoid confrontation with others. Maintain your own humility and avoid embarrassment. Do not miss your chance, look around you carefully for any opportunities (Huang). In this situation ignore others and perfect yourself.

## HEXAGRAM 3

**This hexagram represents: accumulating, waiting and building up slowly**

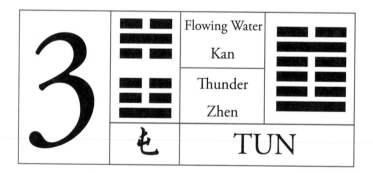

### READ ME FIRST

This hexagram appearing in your casting is a sign that your situation is like a seed sprouting from the earth. You are in the early stages of your development. This is a time for building strength and growing outward. The lower trigram is **Thunder** and the upper trigram is **Flowing Water**.

The image is of difficult times to start with: a storm over rushing water. Therefore, bring all your strength together and face each challenge with controlled determination; do not rush ahead. On the whole this hexagram means to wait and gather strength for a while.

**If you do not have any transforming lines:** take time to build the power you need for any situation. There may be external threats that can strike you down and therefore you need the underlying strength to fight them off. It is best to wait until you are in a stronger position. Move forward slowly and be very careful about what you choose to do. Taking your time is paramount.

**If you do have transforming lines:** consult those lines within this hexagram for a more direct answer. Then transform your hexagram and focus just on the **Read me first** section of the new hexagram to discover what you should do.

### Bottom line
If you have this as a transforming line, lay a solid foundation for everything you do. Put the right people in the right places and build your strength. Pause for a moment to think before you act. It is best to work with other people if you can for a more secure result. In this situation, put all the pieces together like a puzzle before you move.

### Second line up
If you have this as a transforming line, do not jump at any offer. Think first. It might be better to say no at this point and look for the next opportunity. Even if things seem to be falling apart do not just reach for the first thing that comes your way. Also, do not let people force you into a decision you do not want to make. Anyone who comes to help you now may not be the right person; do not begrudge them, but do not rely on them. In this situation, take extra care on the direction you take.

### Third line up
If you have this as a transforming line, look for reliable advice. Going it alone without proper planning may turn out to be a mistake. What seems like a good idea at the start may turn out to be a wrong move. Alternatively, use your instincts to guide you (Adcock) but question your

assumptions, both about the things that you favour and the things that you avoid. Check everything as you may make a mistake if you do not focus (Huang). In this situation, align yourself with other people to make things work.

### Fourth line up

If you have this as a transforming line, now is the time to seize an opportunity. Any offer you have received recently is the correct one. In the past you may have declined offers or gone around in circles waiting. Do not do this anymore. If this is the first offer you have had, take it. All will come out well in the end if you move now. Alternatively, look to accept help from other people (Crisp); or focus on deciding whether to advance or retreat (Huang). It is time to push forward now, but weigh up your options before you choose. In this situation, take people up on what they have to offer.

### Fifth line up

If you have this as a transforming line, do not show too much strength here; take small steps and be patient. If you use too much force you risk damaging existing alliances or scaring new people away. Move cautiously to the next stage; do not overreach yourself. Step back and wait (Huang). Alternatively, people may be out to destroy you so take care (Crisp). In this situation, soft and gentle wins the day.

### Top line

If you have this as a transforming line, ignore any negative aspects at this point. Look for the good in the situation and focus on that. Instead of feeling sorry for yourself or worrying about what to do next, focus on the positives in front of you. Alternatively, trust in fate and it will not fail you (Adcock). Or fate is against you, so retreat (Crisp) or even abandon the situation entirely (Gill). Consider whether this might be as far as you can go with this venture at this time (Huang). In this situation, avoid negativity; look to the positive, but do not plough ahead regardless.

# HEXAGRAM 4

**This hexagram represents: ignorance, undeveloped potential and foolishness**

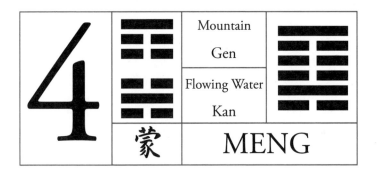

| | | Mountain | | |
| | | Gen | | |
| | | Flowing Water | | |
| | | Kan | | |
| | 蒙 | MENG | | |

READ ME FIRST

This hexagram appearing in your casting indicates that a wise person should instruct the unwise and inexperienced. A heavy reliance on proper structure is needed to grow and there must be a firm understanding between those who know and those who do not know. The lower trigram is **Flowing Water** and the upper trigram is **Mountain**. The image implies that a mountain looks down but takes care of the new growth around it. The original Chinese uses the idea of new grass to represent immaturity or inexperience.

**If you do not have any transforming lines:** poorly developed structures can lead to chaos. There must be rules in place to guide all people. Self-improvement and correct structure are what are needed in your situation.

**If you do have transforming lines:** consult those lines within this hexagram for a more direct answer. Then transform your hexagram and focus just on the **Read me first** section of the new hexagram to discover what you should do.

## Bottom line

If you have this as a transforming line, it is best to reprimand those who are ignorant and show them the correct way so that they do not make mistakes in the future. This is a time to be firm and improve your own discipline and that of others. Accept criticism if it appears to be honest, do not lie, do not cheat and be an example to others (Huang). In this situation, a proper understanding of correct procedure will help everyone.

## Second line up
If you have this as a transforming line, now is the best time to show lenience. Support the people who need it and make sure everyone understands their task. Do not dismiss the views of those without experience and knowledge; they may have new insights and they also need encouragement to find their proper place. Take time to find the correct response; do not leap to a conclusion (Huang). In this situation, everyone has their own talents and their own purpose.

## Third line up
If you have this as a transforming line, be careful of people who want to attach themselves to you for their own profit. Self-seeking people will tend to be disloyal; they will leave you when they see a better opportunity elsewhere. Do not idolize those above you (Adcock) and do not focus on immature desires (Crisp). Try to understand what people's objectives are to see their true nature. In this situation, avoid people who do not feel right.

## Fourth line up
If you have this as a transforming line, keep up to date with what is happening in the world around you. If you stick to old ways you will fall behind. Do not let your ignorance trip you up like tangled undergrowth. Remember, though, even a hard lesson can result in many benefits (Adcock), but do not be deluded by your own ideas (Crisp). Make sure you are free to move without hindrance. In this situation, living in the past is a trap.

## Fifth line up
If you have this as a transforming line, reflect on the idea that sometimes it is better to know too little than too much. Coming to a situation with an open, empty mind is better than being weighed down with outdated ideas. Seek advice from all people, even those not directly connected to the situation. Do not get caught in traps you create for yourself. In this situation, a clear mind works wonders.

**Top line**
If you have this as a transforming line, do not make the first move. If you are being attacked in any way, do not lash out or act in haste. Be defensive. Also, accept what has happened and prepare to move on (Adcock). When setting rules for others, keep in mind that your purpose is to guide them to better behaviour (Crisp). Do not be condescending to those who have less ability than you or who are in an inferior position and do not overreact. In this situation, keep your anger in check.

# HEXAGRAM 5

**This hexagram represents: sincerity, perseverance and calculation**

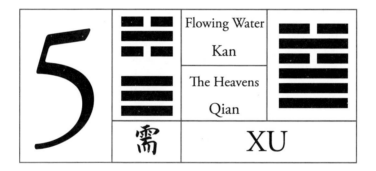

| | | Flowing Water | |
| --- | --- | --- | --- |
| 5 | | Kan | |
| | | The Heavens | |
| | | Qian | |
| | 需 | XU | |

READ ME FIRST

This hexagram appearing in your casting tells you that now is the time to wait, to persevere, to be sincere, to hold back. The lower trigram is **The Heavens** and the upper trigram is **Flowing Water**. The image is of clouds above the earth showering the land with nourishing rain.

**If you do not have any transforming lines:** you may want to rush forward but now is the time for ground work. Know that deciding not to act is itself an action. Some parts of this hexagram talk about looking for opportunity and moving if you have already been waiting, but on the whole it is best to stand fast. No matter how good or bad your situation is, just stay where you are and maintain a solid, secure position.

**If you do have transforming lines:** consult those lines within this hexagram for a more direct answer. Then transform your hexagram and focus just on the **Read me first** section of the new hexagram to discover what you should do.

### Bottom line
If you have this as a transforming line, know that waiting on the fringes is better than putting yourself in the middle of the action. Stay away from anyone who is a threat at this time and wait until the situation changes. Appreciate what you have at the present. In this situation, it is better to wait on the outside of the situation.

### Second line up
If you have this as a transforming line, think of your situation as being like standing barefoot on baking hot sand. Even though this is a little uncomfortable, it is better to wait here than to move to what could be a worse situation. Would you prefer to be a little too hot or freeze to death? Use this time to build momentum without anyone noticing and do not respond hastily to attacks. Take all the precautions you can to stay in a solid position at this time (Gill). In this situation, your position, though not ideal, is better than it could be if you make the wrong move.

### Third line up
If you have this as a transforming line, it is as if you are stuck in mud. Being stuck like this makes you vulnerable to attack, but there are worse situations you could be in. Beware of becoming isolated from those who can support you; find allies to protect you. Look for a good way out of this situation (Crisp), use your inner calmness to find strength (Adcock) and prepare for attacks from the outside (Gill). Take extra care here because not all is positive in the direction you are heading (Huang). In this situation, avoid opening yourself up to danger.

### Fourth line up
If you have this as a transforming line, think of yourself as trapped in a dangerous cave or pit. Things may become threatening. Now is the time to act if needs be or to wait; either way be very cautious and look out for danger. Forget whatever else you are doing and prepare to defend yourself

with all your heart. However, remain calm and confident (Adcock). In this situation, be extremely vigilant.

### Fifth line up

If you have this as a transforming line, know that even though you are in a stable, comfortable position, you still need to keep persevering. You are in the right place for now, but keep your eye out for an even better opening. To move now would be detrimental, so hold tight. Enjoy the things you have and use this time to build your strength. There is a moral path through the situation you are in, but you have to find it (Huang). In this situation, stay on your current path but knuckle down.

### Top line

If you have this as a transforming line, welcome all people at this stage. If something unexpected happens, embrace it and go with the flow. Treat anyone who approaches you with kindness, as they may help you. Even though it might not be the outcome you want, the situation you are in is coming to an end (Adcock). Be ready for something to happen (Gill). In this situation, now is a good time but enjoy what comes next while keeping your eyes open for any pitfalls.

## HEXAGRAM 6

**This hexagram represents: strife, conflict, caution, justice and resolution**

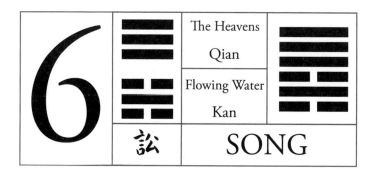

| 6 | ☰ | The Heavens Qian | ☰ |
| | ☵ | Flowing Water Kan | ☵ |
| | 訟 | SONG | |

READ ME FIRST

This hexagram appearing in your casting represents an attempt to cross a great river. It is far more powerful than you are and you will fail if you push yourself too far. The lower trigram is **Flowing Water** and the upper trigram is **The Heavens**. This represents an overwhelming situation, like being exposed to extreme weather or caught in a strong current.

**If you do not have any transforming lines:** do not start proceedings at this time. If there is a battle to be fought, wait; the opposing forces will be too powerful for you. Now is not the time to fight. If there is an issue that needs to be resolved, seek a compromise.

**If you do have transforming lines:** consult those lines within this hexagram for a more direct answer. Then transform your hexagram and focus just on the **Read me first** section of the new hexagram to discover what you should do.

## Bottom line

If you have this as a transforming line, know that if you are facing an argument or battle of some kind you should make people aware of your plight, but do not fight head on. Do not worry about being seen to shy away from a fight; it is better to try to take the heat out of the situation. Lie low and wait for the moment to move (Huang). In this situation, do not engage with the argument; let people know you are in trouble but do not force the issue.

## Second line up

If you have this as a transforming line, choose your battles wisely and do not fight against an opponent you cannot defeat. Shelter with your supporters, even if there are not many of them. Pull away from any potential conflict and keep your head down. Pushing forward out of spite or anger will not help. In this situation, avoid any battles unless you are sure you can win.

## Third line up

If you have this as a transforming line, return to your stronghold and gather your strength. Now is the time to retreat to safety and find support from others. Focus on fulfilling your role, not moving beyond it. When you are stronger you can try again, but in the meantime wait with calmness and forbearance. In this situation, withdraw to a secure position.

### Fourth line up

If you have this as a transforming line, do not fight against the flow. To go against overwhelming odds is foolishness. Stand and wait or put your energies into something else. Just accept the situation. Rethink your original ideas; they may not be correct (Huang). In this situation, you might be on the wrong path; maybe you need to look for a better way.

### Fifth line up

If you have this as a transforming line, seek help from the people around you in resolving your dilemma. Find someone you trust to listen to your problems. If those in power agree with you the issue will be overcome (Crisp). In this situation, look for support from people you trust.

### Top line

If you have this as a transforming line, know that any recognition you have previously received may be taken away. Do not seek reward or validation from others. A victory now may lead to defeat later. If you continue to push your point now, you may win in the short term but make yourself a target in the future. In this situation, pushing too hard may cause you to lose the ground you have gained.

## HEXAGRAM 7

**This hexagram represents organization, disciplined groups, followers, unity and order**

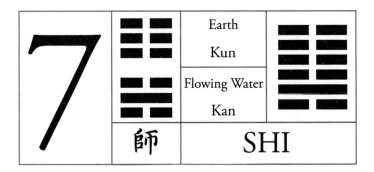

| 7 | Earth Kun |  |
|---|---|---|
|  | Flowing Water Kan |  |
|  | 師 | SHI |

READ ME FIRST

This hexagram appearing in your casting represents strict protocols, proper organization and rigidity. People need leadership, direction and a cause, so give it to them. The lower trigram is **Flowing Water** and the upper trigram is **Earth**. The idea is that all the rivers and water courses upon the earth form a well-organized system of natural irrigation. Everything has its place in the world and can be marshalled into a force of nature. Therefore, organize yourself.

**If you do not have any transforming lines:** make sure that you and the people around you are organized. Do not give power to the wrong people, reward the faithful and make sure everyone, including yourself, clearly understands the situation and how you are going to deal with it.

**If you do have transforming lines:** consult those lines within this hexagram for a more direct answer. Then transform your hexagram and focus just on the **Read me first** section of the new hexagram to discover what you should do.

### Bottom line

If you have this as a transforming line, make sure the right people are in the right positions; there must be proper organization in all you do. Focus on the proper set up in this situation and behave in the correct manner. Examine and re-examine all possible options before you move forward (Huang). In this situation, organization and planning are the key to success.

### Second line up

If you have this as a transforming line, focus on your own efforts; make sure that everything you do is correct and well organized. Whether you are the leader or a follower, establish orderly relationships between members of the group and do not let any disagreements fester. Be centred or lead from the centre and share hardships with others to gain their trust. In this situation, get everything in order before you start.

### Third line up

If you have this as a transforming line, you may be about to make a disastrous mistake. Rethink your plans. Be realistic about your abilities and maintain command over the situation. Do not engage with unworthy people and guard against any signs of incompetence around you. In this situation, get rid of those things which do not benefit you.

### Fourth line up

If you have this as a transforming line, find a place to retreat to. Moving forward at this point would be a mistake. There has to be coherence between yourself and other people but also within your own mind. Find a safe place and stay away from opponents much stronger than you. In this situation, defence is the best form of attack.

### Fifth line up

If you have this as a transforming line, even if you are in a strong position do not push forward. You may have had some form of victory but if you keep pushing forward now you will fail. Approach all encounters in a spirit of peace, avoid aggression and do not move into an unprotected position. Alternatively, move forward and take your chance (Crisp), but do not involve too many people in the decision-making or you will tumble into confusion (Huang). In this situation, do not retreat but if you advance do so with great care.

### Top line

If you have this as a transforming line, now is the time to make sure that everyone is doing what they should be, including yourself. Titles and honours given to undeserving people are worthless. If you are in a position of power be honest about how you gained it and what you intend to do with it. Be very careful not to give power to the wrong people, but make sure to share any rewards you get with people who have been faithful to you. Do not let anyone of inferior ability take control. In this situation, do not be fooled by people who say they can but cannot – yourself included.

# HEXAGRAM 8

**This hexagram represents alliances, bonding, cooperation and closeness**

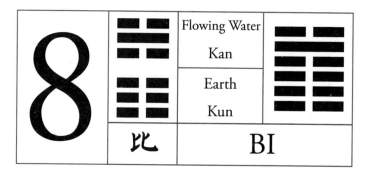

| | | Flowing Water | |
| :-: | :-: | :-- | :-: |
| **8** | | Kan | |
| | | Earth | |
| | | Kun | |
| | 比 | BI | |

**READ ME FIRST**

This hexagram appearing in your casting represents alliances, the coming together of different groups and mutually beneficial actions. The lower trigram is **Earth** and the upper trigram is **Flowing Water**, which conveys the idea of two aspects of nature working together: water soaks into the ground and creates the conditions for a good harvest.

**If you do not have any transforming lines:** get into a group for support, make sure there is fairness and never pressure people to join the group or force those already in the group to stay. Everyone is in the group to support each other, but it needs good leadership and clear goals.

**If you do have transforming lines:** consult those lines within this hexagram for a more direct answer. Then transform your hexagram and focus just on the **Read me first** section of the new hexagram to discover what you should do.

## Bottom line

If you have this as a transforming line, find trustworthy people to support you and ensure that you have a genuine concern for other people. If you do this, things will work out better for you. Also, make sure to keep a sense of justice. If you are sincere throughout you will come off the better. In this situation, bond well with the people who support you and pay special attention to the relationships around you at this time.

### Second line up

If you have this as a transforming line, now may be the time to make an alliance with people you once considered to be enemies. Stay honest and build friendships with people you would not normally expect to have dealings with. In this situation, keep any existing groups together while also forming friendships with new people – even people you would not expect to work with.

### Third line up

If you have this as a transforming line, this is a time to turn an enemy into a friend. People whom you least expect to help you might do so if the conditions are mutually beneficial. Find an unlikely ally but maintain a degree of authority without being overbearing (Adcock). Consider whether the people around you at the moment are the right ones (Gill and Crisp). Alternatively, now is not the time to unite with new people (Huang). In this situation, give serious thought to joining with someone totally unexpected, but only do so if the arrangement suits both parties.

### Fourth line up

If you have this as a transforming line, now is the time to make friends and alliances with people not connected to the issue at hand. Look for help in unexpected places. Follow a coherent strategy with honesty and perseverance. Also, show the people around you that you trust them (Crisp). In this situation, look for a solution in unconventional places.

### Fifth line up

If you have this as a transforming line, do not force any alliances. If people do not want to join or help you, or if there is a situation where there is a conflict, do not force anyone else to share your opinion. Let people do as they wish or be as they want to be. Although the present situation may be disrupting what you want to do, do not come down like a hammer on it; be gentle in how you approach any problems at hand. Do not force people away through overbearing behaviour and be fair in all your actions (Crisp). In this situation, seek help but do not demand it.

### Top line

If you have this as a transforming line, great leadership is needed. If you do not currently have a leader or you have the wrong kind of leader, try to find a person who will genuinely look for the best option and not exploit the situation for their own benefit. Try to find the correct way to deal with the issue with an honest heart. Give people a clear purpose. Reflect honestly on the situation to see how you got here and know that if you do not find support at this juncture you may fail (Gill). Also, set off on the right foot; a wrong move at the start will damage your cause (Crisp). In this situation, focus on strong, unselfish leadership and give people a goal to aim for.

## HEXAGRAM 9

**This hexagram represents small progressions, a turning point and restraint**

| | Wind Xun | |
|---|---|---|
| 9 | The Heavens Qian | |
| 小畜 | XIAO XU | |

**READ ME FIRST**

This hexagram appearing in your casting means that it is almost time to make a move, so prepare yourself for what you must do. The lower trigram is **The Heavens** and the upper trigram is **Wind**, meaning that the wind is gusting high above the clouds and that movement on the ground is almost there, but not quite yet. It is the breeze that moves the leaves before the storm hits.

**If you do not have any transforming lines:** do not rush forward. Maintain small, steady steps in the direction you want to go. Do not stand still or retreat, just make sure you do not push forward too hard. Moving too early will cause you to falter.

**If you do have transforming lines:** consult those lines within this hexagram for a more direct answer. Then transform your hexagram and focus just on the **Read me first** section of the new hexagram to discover what you should do.

### Bottom line
If you have this as a transforming line, look for the small victories. Do not go for the main goal at the moment but instead take the win you can then retreat back into safety and comfort. If you push too far outward it will become a problem. Do not be hasty, move slowly and make sure to readjust and find the best path (Huang). In this situation, if you focus on small wins you will gain more ground than trying to overreach for the bigger issue.

### Second line up
If you have this as a transforming line, now is the time to thank and reward the people who have helped you. This will smooth the situation you are in. Share any rewards with others who deserve it and remain focused on your purpose (Adcock). Also, search for an alternative way to do things instead of pushing on with your current ideas (Crisp). If people you trust are trying to restrain you, listen to them because it may be for the best (Gill). Finally, make life easier for yourself by sharing the burden with other people (Huang). In this situation, telling people how much you appreciate what they have done for you will ease your path.

### Third line up
If you have this as a transforming line, do not argue with anyone at this point and do not allow arguments between other people to happen. If there is any discord do not allow it to get worse; like a cart with no brakes the situation risks running out of control. Banish any doubts from your mind, as they will not help you (Adcock). Also, build a strong alliance with someone who thinks similarly to you (Huang). In this situation, avoid all arguments and find like-minded people who will not cause trouble.

### Fourth line up
If you have this as a transforming line, remember that sometimes you have to go through bad times to get to where you need to be. There may be trouble ahead, but do what you can to limit the damage and do not

cause any more damage through being too aggressive. Accept that you may have to back down to avoid conflict, even if you are in the right. Now is the time to be honest about any problems, straighten things out and accept support from other people (Huang). In this situation, be prepared to ride out tough times and do not look for any more trouble than you are already in.

## Fifth line up

If you have this as a transforming line, keep your heart in it, do not give up and recognize people who are supporting you. Show companionship and love for all and press on with what you want to do. If you continue to be loving, others will support you because they see your honesty and enthusiasm. Sharing your effort and time now will increase your power and attract others to you. Spread the rewards around. In this situation, show your enthusiasm to others and show people you are enthusiastic about them.

## Top line

If you have this as a transforming line, even though you have had small victories, it is not quite time to launch forward in earnest. Resist any urge to leap ahead, or to retreat. Now is the time to move slowly but steadily forward, sharing your thoughts with others and building momentum. You are almost there, so do not ruin things now by being impatient. If you are in a position of victory, settle down and relax, otherwise your success may be short-lived (Crisp). In this situation, do not push too hard but do not retreat.

# HEXAGRAM 10

**This hexagram represents treading, testing and cautious movement**

| 10 | The Heavens Qian | |
| | Still Water Dui | |
| 履 | LU | |

This hexagram appearing in your casting suggests that you should test the limits of your power. If you stand on a tiger's tale and the tiger does not turn on you, you can tell it is unsure how strong you are. This means that, even though the situation may be difficult, you can move forward at this point, but do so with caution until you understand who has the real power. The lower trigram is **Still Water** and the upper trigram is **The Heavens**. The image here is of a great expanse before you that may hold many hidden dangers, so you need to proceed with small steps until you have tested what is out there.

**If you do not have any transforming lines:** take small steps to probe the situation you are in. Try not to change your approach too much from what you have done in the past. Look at the situation with an honest heart and do not fool yourself. Be flexible even if you are moving forward very slowly.

**If you do have transforming lines:** consult those lines within this hexagram for a more direct answer. Then transform your hexagram and focus just on the **Read me first** section of the new hexagram to discover what you should do.

### Bottom line

If you have this as a transforming line, it is time to move forward and engage with your issue, but take a familiar path. Do not try to push too far forward, or too quickly, or in a direction that you do not know. Also, be happy with your progress so far (Crisp) and make sure to fulfil all your duties and follow up on all responsibilities so that you can clear the way ahead (Huang). In this situation, keep doing what you normally do and move forward slowly and gently.

### Second line up

If you have this as a transforming line, now is a time to look within yourself. Focus on the issue at hand and move forward by yourself with determination. This does not mean you should get rid of any support structure you have in place, but it means that you have what you need already within you. Do what you know to be correct in your heart (Adcock) and keep everything on the straight and level (Gill). In this situation, move forward in your own way and stay focused on getting where you want to go.

### Third line up

If you have this as a transforming line, make sure that your plan is watertight. Check everything before moving forward. In this situation, be honest with yourself, do not overestimate your ability and make sure that your goal is realistic.

### Fourth line up

If you have this as a transforming line, understand that there is no need to hold back, but do not overreach. Move forward little by little but with enough power to test the waters. If the situation is too difficult to deal with, do not push it but likewise do not give in too easily. In this situation, do not pretend to be strong if you are not and be honest about your own abilities.

### Fifth line up

If you have this as a transforming line, you must be prepared at this time. Avoid complacency and inflexibility; you may need to make adjustments. Also, do not judge others too harshly (Adcock). Work with any changes that arise or, alternatively, understand that you are on the correct path but know it may be a little dangerous (Gill). Overall, this is a good position from which to move into action (Huang). In this situation, make the small adjustments you need, be flexible, avoid any obvious dangers and move forward with your ideas.

## Top line

If you have this as a transforming line, now is the time to examine what worked in the past and what did not work. Pick tried and tested strategies and go on to the next stage. If you gain a victory it is extremely important to take note of how you went about it (Adcock). In this situation, remember what worked in the past and apply it here.

# HEXAGRAM 11

**This hexagram represents: prominence and bursting energy**

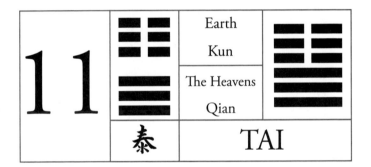

| 11 | ☷ | Earth<br>Kun | ☷ |
| | ☰ | The Heavens<br>Qian | |
| | 泰 | TAI | |

READ ME FIRST

This hexagram appearing in your casting indicates that the situation you are in revolves around prominence, eminence and abundance. Great things are about to arrive, while negativity and unwanted aspects will take their leave. The lower trigram is **The Heavens** and the upper trigram is **Earth**. The image is that of the heavens preparing to burst up through the ground, which promises great potential if you can maintain balance. It is as though heaven is on earth around you or heaven and earth are in harmony.

**If you do not have any transforming lines:** whatever you are doing is correct and you should keep doing it. You may feel as if you are suffering setbacks, but you are actually making good progress. Maintain true balance at this time. Keep your focus and push on, but avoid favouritism and weed out any negative aspects before they grow into problems.

**If you do have transforming lines:** consult those lines within this hexagram for a more direct answer. Then transform your hexagram and focus just on the **Read me first** section of the new hexagram to discover what you should do.

### Bottom line

If you have this as a transforming line, look to eradicate all negativity around you. This includes staying away from negative people. If people are attracted by your success share it with them but also clear the way for better growth. A new start may be a blessing in disguise (Gill). Also, look for like-minded people who are attracted to you (Crisp). In this situation, it is time to strip away everything in your life that is causing you problems.

### Second line up

If you have this as a transforming line, do not give preference to friends or reward the unworthy. Now is the time to put the best person in the best position. If you play favourites or give your attention to the wrong people things will go astray. Do not allow success to cloud your judgement and be fair in all matters. Understand which people are close and which are at a distance. In this situation, value those around you for their real worth, not what they say they are worth.

### Third line up

If you have this as a transforming line, appreciate the good things that you have. Hold tight when things get difficult, and know that the good times will return if you maintain your course. Sustaining a proper attitude in both success and defeat will burnish your reputation. Remember, what goes up must come down; it is the natural order of things. In this situation, go with the flow, sustain a positive attitude and push on through the situation you are in.

### Fourth line up

If you have this as a transforming line, you have arrived at success. There is something fantastic before you that you need to grab hold of. Use the correct people to put everything into place but do not let success go to your head. No one likes to see that. Be kind and fair to people who are less successful than you; harmonious relationships are more valuable than a reward for which you are resented. Keep any relationships you have in a state of peace and do not flit from person to person (Huang). In this situation, maintain a level head, treat people with respect and give them your attention.

**Fifth line up**
If you have this as a transforming line, you have to ally yourself with the correct person. There is someone out there who is perfectly equipped to help you achieve your aim. If you find this person you will bring many other people together and create a positive situation. Maintain inner calmness and do not worry; things are just as they should be (Adcock). In this situation, build the correct team and keep going; you are on the right path.

**Top line**
If you have this as a transforming line, build trust, openness and solidarity from the inside. Something within yourself or your team is not right at the moment and you need to find out what it is. If your fortunes are fading keep calm and focus on repairing that which is damaged. Return to the centre and take stock. In this situation, stop the rot before it spreads.

# HEXAGRAM 12

**This hexagram represents: adversity, blockage and stagnation**

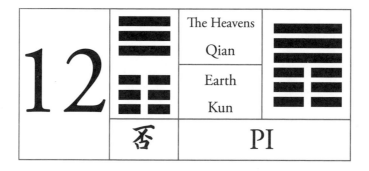

| 12 | The Heavens Qian | | |
|---|---|---|---|
| | Earth Kun | | |
| | 否 | PI | |

READ ME FIRST

This hexagram appearing in your casting means that there is an obstruction or difficulty present now. There is something blocking your progress at this point so that people with lesser ability are succeeding where you are not. The lower trigram is **Earth** and the upper trigram is **The Heavens**. The image is that of the earth and the sky not moving. There is a sense of stagnation, like on a windless day.

**If you do not have any transforming lines:** this period of stagnation is not your fault. You cannot do anything about all these barriers and people who want to stop you. You can move forward but you will need to clear the way first. Investigate your situation and see what or who is blocking your path. Alternatively, the path you have chosen may be too difficult and this may be why you are not making much progress. If things are going wrong around you, stand firm and hold on to your morality.

**If you do have transforming lines:** consult those lines within this hexagram for a more direct answer. Then transform your hexagram and focus just on the **Read me first** section of the new hexagram to discover what you should do.

**Bottom line**

If you have this as a transforming line, free yourself from corrupt and negative people. There is someone or something blocking your way. Remove them or it to progress. It is best that you step away from any negative situations and wait for times to change (Adcock) and when times do change you will move forward with no problems if you have been positive (Crisp). Be sincere with the people around you for better clarity (Huang). In this situation, you will gain benefit from correct action.

**Second line up**

If you have this as a transforming line, inferior people may prosper at this time. Do not flatter people and do not fall for flattery. Surround yourself with genuine people. Also, do not push away anyone who is honest with you just because you do not like what they say. Endure everything with patience and do not be discouraged (Adcock). If people around you are gaining favour through lying, do not be tempted to copy them; your honesty will win through in the end (Gill). In this situation, do not worry if the unworthy seem to be getting ahead; your time will come.

### Third line up

If you have this as a transforming line, someone or something is deceiving you and there is hidden malice around you at this time. Listen carefully to what people say. Make sure that their words match their actions and identify those who are false. Someone is hiding a shameful act or being deceitful in some way. Alternatively, do not judge others (Adcock); endure any shame you may have to face if you can (Gill); and correct any mistakes you have made (Crisp). Do not conceal anything shameful from people (Huang). In this situation, dishonesty may be causing harm; find the source of the deceit and make sure you are being honest.

### Fourth line up

If you have this as a transforming line, now is the time to correct any injustices or imperfections in your situation. Act in accordance with the honest nature of heaven and make changes for the better. Act with sincerity and good people will help you (Adcock). Find benefits for all people involved to help you move through this time (Crisp) and follow good advice from trustworthy people (Gill). In this situation, focus on those who you can trust and look to make changes for the benefit of everyone.

### Fifth line up

If you have this as a transforming line, there is a way out of this period of stagnation. Stick close to sincere people who will help you push forward. If you stay on the honourable path then you will overcome any obstructions standing in your way. Stick to your principles and strengthen your inner resolve. It is time to move from inaction to action (Crisp), but make sure your deeds take root like seeds growing slowly but surely in the ground (Gill). In this situation, look for an opening and you will find one.

### Top line

If you have this as a transforming line, any stagnation you are suffering is coming to an end. It is time to remove any barriers remaining in your mind or within the situation so that you can move forward. If you stay honest you will prosper (Adcock). A big push now will end your troubles (Gill). In this situation, it is time to smash through that final obstacle.

# HEXAGRAM 13

**This hexagram represents: gathering, fellowship, union and friendship**

| 13 | (trigram) | The Heavens<br>Qian<br>Fire<br>Li | (hexagram) |
|---|---|---|---|
| | 同人 | TONG REN | |

**READ ME FIRST**

This hexagram appearing in your casting represents people gathering together and alliances being formed. The lower trigram is **Fire** and the upper trigram is **The Heavens**. This represents the light of the world spreading out into the sky, just as the bonds you are building reach out into the community around you.

**If you do not have any transforming lines:** gather your forces and supporters quietly and start to build up a unified strength. Find people to help you but do not let people realize what you are doing or invite the wrong people in. Unity is the key to success. You should also treat all people well, whether they are friends or foes. Forming bonds with people will benefit you at this point in your journey. You need to focus on friendship, and keeping relationships positive.

**If you do have transforming lines:** consult those lines within this hexagram for a more direct answer. Then transform your hexagram and focus just on the **Read me first** section of the new hexagram to discover what you should do.

**Bottom line**

If you have this as a transforming line, look around you for alliances that are not so obvious. Be open to all people, including those you do not know well or even at all (Adcock) and welcome new friends (Gill). Do not close yourself off (Crisp). In this situation find support from both expected and unexpected places.

## Second line up

If you have this as a transforming line, know that if you only look for help from the obvious people you will regret it. Expand your focus. Also, if you create factions within your allies (Adcock) or fail to stop factions forming (Gill), things will end badly. Selfishness and fragmentation will lead to disaster (Crisp and Huang). In this situation, stop any division and look for help in different places.

## Third line up

If you have this as a transforming line, find a concealed place from which to observe your opponent and wait for the best time to move. But also observe your allies, because if you let distrust form between any members of your group there will be problems (Adcock). By handling the situation wrongly at this point you will become stuck for a long time (Gill). Therefore, watch out for any enemies who may infiltrate your cause (Crisp). In this situation, look out for negative people influencing your group and observe your opponent closely until you see your opportunity.

## Fourth line up

If you have this as a transforming line, now is the time to show fairness and sportsmanship. Do not push anyone too far, or you will lose respect. Disengage from any troubles for an easier future (Gill and Crisp). Avoid anything shocking and controversial (Huang). In this situation be fair, do not force anything, avoid trouble and keep a low profile.

## Fifth line up

If you have this as a transforming line, hold a small celebration. Find time to relax and reflect on what you have achieved so far. Appreciate the people who have helped you to ensure their continuing support and love. Look back on the good times and the bad in order to process what you have done. If a situation starts in anger and tears make sure it ends in friendship and laughter (Gill). In this situation, focus on the people around you and relive your past with them to help strengthen the bonds between you.

**Top line**

If you have this as a transforming line, show compassion to others, especially your opponents. Think hard about the effect your actions have on the people around you. If possible, seek advice from someone wiser than you (Adcock), but to invite the wrong people into your confidence would be a disaster (Gill). Spend time with people who matter (Crisp) and be content with where you have got to (Huang). In this situation, do no actions that will damage anyone involved with you and keep the wrong people away from your inner circle.

## HEXAGRAM 14

**This hexagram represents: great rewards, possessions and plentifulness**

| 14 | Fire |
|---|---|
| | Li |
| | The Heavens |
| | Qian |
| 大有 | DA YOU |

READ ME FIRST

This hexagram appearing in your casting means that what you are doing or have done is or was a good move, and it deserves rewards. The lower trigram is **The Heavens** and the upper trigram is **Fire**. This gives an image of bright light high up in the sky shining down on the crops to make them grow and bringing an abundance of wealth. It is a time of radiance and brilliance for you.

**If you do not have any transforming lines:** you are in a period of prosperity and you are on the right track. Accept your good fortune with humility. Although this is a good time for you now, tread carefully.

**If you do have transforming lines:** consult those lines within this hexagram for a more direct answer. Then transform your hexagram and focus just on the **Read me first** section of the new hexagram to discover what you should do.

## Bottom line

If you have this as a transforming line, be aware of any hidden difficulties that may be lurking. Do not underestimate any opponents or obstacles around you. Also, do not become arrogant (Adcock) or let the situation go to your head (Crisp) or be overly proud (Huang). In this situation, take extra care to check for dangers and do not let your pride get the better of you.

## Second line up

If you have this as a transforming line, make sure you have everything you need to make your next move. Check your equipment, funding and supplies. Only make that move once you are sure you have what is necessary. Alternatively, share your wealth – be it spiritual, emotional or physical – with people who need it (Crisp), and do not become attached to material things (Adcock). There is a way for you to go forward if you follow these principles (Huang). In this situation, check whether you have the resources to go for your goal, or help others achieve theirs.

## Third line up

If you have this as a transforming line, you are in for a reward. Look around you for anything that is moving in your favour and see this as your prize for getting this far. Only superb people can move forward; make sure you are one of them. Avoid hoarding wealth, which can lead to stagnation (Adcock). Share your wealth (Crisp) with the people who need it most, not the people whom you think will benefit you most (Gill). In this situation, be encouraged by any rewards that come your way, while also rewarding people of merit with your time and resources.

## Fourth line up

If you have this as a transforming line, be warned that you must stay humble at this time. Do not boast or push yourself forward, as this will irritate others. Stay away from petty matters (Adcock) and be content with where you are (Crisp). In this situation, realize there are times when you just have to wait and never forget that you have a lot left to learn.

### Fifth line up

If you have this as a transforming line, be careful how you treat those who are in a lesser position. If you treat them with kindness you will benefit; if you look down on them you will miss out. The way people think of you depends on the way you treat them. In this situation, respect will be rewarded and arrogance will be punished.

### Top line

If you have this as a transforming line, know that the heavens support what you are doing now. If you stay humble and honest people will celebrate any success that you end up achieving (Crisp and Huang). In this situation, you are on the right path so keep going.

## HEXAGRAM 15

**This hexagram represents: modesty and moderation**

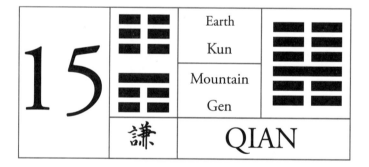

| 15 | Earth<br>Kun | |
| | Mountain<br>Gen | |
| | 謙 | QIAN |

READ ME FIRST

This hexagram appearing in your casting means that you should try to be modest and take a less prominent role in your current situation. Put your head down for a while. The lower trigram is **Mountain** and the upper trigram is **Earth**. This gives an image of a mountain not protruding too far above the surrounding landscape. It needs the support of the earth below it to stay firm.

**If you do not have any transforming lines:** whether you are already in a good position or are trying to achieve one, stay modest and do not over-assert yourself. That does not mean you should disappear from view, it just means you should not be too pushy in whatever situation you are in. Keep a humble attitude or you will alienate people.

**If you do have transforming lines:** consult those lines within this hexagram for a more direct answer. Then transform your hexagram and focus just on the **Read me first** section of the new hexagram to discover what you should do.

### Bottom line

If you have this as a transforming line, it is a warning not to boast about your abilities. Doing so will close doors of opportunity in your face. Stay quiet and move forward in a reserved manner and understand that now is not the time to look for reward (Adcock). Alternatively, do not make any promises you cannot keep (Crisp). In this situation, avoid being brash, check what you say and how you say it, and do not press anyone to give you something, be it time, emotional support or resources.

### Second line up

If you have this as a transforming line, you should not push your claims too hard. Over-promoting yourself will backfire. Alternatively, stand firm and be seen for who you are (Gill) and express your point with quiet assertiveness (Crisp). In this situation, move forward without drawing attention to yourself.

### Third line up

If you have this as a transforming line, it is time for you to stay in the background but still work hard. A successful person is both hardworking and humble. However, do not become complacent. Avoid daydreaming about putting ideas into action. In this situation, you should focus on any loose ends that need to be tied up or preparations that need to be made before you set off toward your goal.

### Fourth line up

If you have this as a transforming line, follow the example of people who are able to glide through situations smoothly and avoid copying those who are brash and irritating. Find someone to guide you in the art of diplomacy. You should still make some movements toward your goal but do so with caution (Gill) and work quietly and persistently (Adcock). In this situation, emulate people who succeed with honesty and humility.

### Fifth line up

If you have this as a transforming line, it means that your supporters may abandon you if you do not recognize their efforts. Show them that you care by sharing your wealth, whether monetary or spiritual, with them. Do not be overzealous in anything you do at this time. Remember that being modest does not mean being weak (Crisp) and if you have to assert yourself do it with a quiet determination (Adcock). In this situation, be strong, be firm, but be generous.

### Top line

If you have this as a transforming line, welcome all people, no matter who they are. Showing genuine kindness and understanding to people will gain you allies and advance your interests. Alternatively, be energetic with people in the things you do (Gill) but maintain discipline at this time (Crisp) and double check what is correct and what is not for this time (Adcock). In this situation, be kind and welcoming to all while maintaining good discipline, and think before you do anything.

## HEXAGRAM 16

**This hexagram represents: satisfaction, enthusiasm and excess**

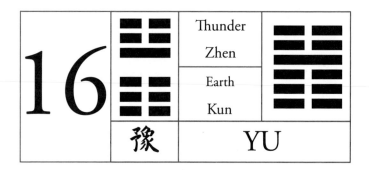

This hexagram appearing in your casting means that you need to focus either on satisfying yourself or satisfying others. The lower trigram is **Earth** and the upper trigram is **Thunder**. This image conveys the idea that the earth is shaking with thunder; it can even represent an earthquake. Pearson sees this as an animated movement, which in moderation brings enjoyment but in excess can be detrimental. Huang states that thunder resounds for miles around and fills the land.

**If you do not have any transforming lines:** the key here is understanding what it will take right now to be happy or bring happiness to others. This may be a time of positivity or success but it can lead to trouble because too much of anything is negative. Also, you may need help to gain the satisfaction you require but do not let this reduce your momentum. Whether things are going well or badly, keep going. Do not rest at this time.

**If you do have transforming lines:** consult those lines within this hexagram for a more direct answer. Then transform your hexagram and focus just on the **Read me first** section of the new hexagram to discover what you should do.

### Bottom line

If you have this as a transforming line, it means that you are in danger of becoming overconfident, of failing to see your true position within the situation, which may cause you to slacken off. Therefore, now is the time to check your true state of mind and do not boast or annoy people. You have got a long way to go, so do not burn out with overexcitement (Huang). In this situation, you should settle your mind, watch what you say and do not get ahead of yourself.

### Second line up

If you have this as a transforming line, think about whether there are any people, situations or problems stopping you from moving forward with your plans? If so, focus on circumventing these barriers. Be prudent yet firm in your convictions and aims because now is a good time for you; enjoy it (Crisp). Recognize which things you can actually achieve and which you only *think* you can achieve (Adcock). You must identify the difference between right and wrong here (Huang). In this situation, go around obstacles rather than trying to fight your way over them.

### Third line up

If you have this as a transforming line, do not wait to move on with your plans. If you stop now you will lose momentum. Think deeply to understand what is the best thing to do. Do not be distracted by superficial ideas (Adcock) and do not let others put you down (Crisp). Avoid wallowing in any victories you may have won because it will stop your forward movement (Huang). In this situation, you should maintain your progress, delve ever deeper into your mind to find any ideas to help at this time and do not let anyone stop you.

### Fourth line up

If you have this as a transforming line, do not let any doubts come into your mind about what you have just done or what you are about to do. What you have in mind is correct. Celebrate what you have achieved so far and where you are heading and bring people together to make your plans a reality (Gill). Alternatively, use allies who are in a good position to help you make your move (Crisp) and take comfort in friendship. In this situation, trust your gut instinct and enlist other people to help you move toward your goal.

### Fifth line up

If you have this as a transforming line, it means you should correct any mistakes which you may have made. Do whatever you can to rectify the situation immediately. Have the confidence to be honest about your failures or mistakes. Like a good medicine, this will restore balance. Even if you are feeling completely burnt out, push on a little more (Huang). In this situation, make amends for anything you have done wrong, do not try to excuse yourself, and bring back harmony to your life and relationships before they go off course.

### Top line

If you have this as a transforming line, it means it is time to make a change. This hexagram is about satisfaction; if you dwell on past glories your satisfaction will fade. Look for a new challenge, or a new angle within your current aims. Identify the best outlet for your efforts before it is too late. Open your eyes to your true situation, not the one you imagine (Crisp). Do not follow an egotistical path; stay centred in reality (Adcock). In this situation, make new memories, set new goals, go out into the world and seek new opportunities.

# HEXAGRAM 17

**This hexagram represents: following and accompanying**

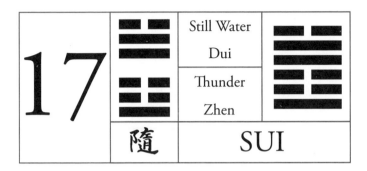

| 17 | ䷐ | Still Water Dui | ䷐ |
| | | Thunder Zhen | |
| | 隨 | SUI | |

READ ME FIRST

This hexagram appearing in your casting represents following through, keeping a promise or continuing on the same course while following correct action. The lower trigram is **Thunder** and the upper trigram is **Still Water**. The image is of movement over a lake creating ripples. The ripples follow the same direction, which evokes the idea of accompanying.

**If you do not have any transforming lines:** it might be time for you to follow someone else's example or follow a particular direction that opens up to you. Following here does not mean following blindly; it means following the correct path, so take care to find it.

**If you do have transforming lines:** consult those lines within this hexagram for a more direct answer. Then transform your hexagram and focus just on the **Read me first** section of the new hexagram to discover what you should do.

## Bottom line

If you have this as a transforming line, you need to solidify your position, find people to help you and take control of the situation correctly. Look for a new path that may open up to you (Gill). Get out and explore and talk to the right people (Crisp). Look for wisdom or advice from unexpected places (Adcock) and know that fortune is found in following only that which is correct (Huang). In this situation, seek advice from new sources and engage with new things to find a new way to your goal.

### Second line up

If you have this as a transforming line, avoid getting involved in anything that deep down you know is wrong. If it does not feel right, it is not right. Find people, situations or pursuits that are strong and helpful and not weak and useless (Crisp). Understand that if you are not open to the truth you will not be able to hear it (Adcock), so if you are going to follow a leader choose wisely (Huang). In this situation, listen to your conscience; refusing to address what you know to be wrong is stopping you progressing.

### Third line up

If you have this as a transforming line, focus on positive elements within yourself and other people. The more you align yourself with what is correct and good, the less evil and negativity will be attracted to you. Do not hesitate to detach yourself from situations or people you perceive to be negative (Adcock). In this situation, start afresh and follow a more righteous path to get where you need to be.

### Fourth line up

If you have this as a transforming line, take an honest look at your situation. Look for malign intentions lurking beneath apparently well-meaning exteriors. Threats may come from other people or yourself. Be careful; there may be evil about, so act decisively after you have fully investigated the situation (Gill). Stick to what is true. Do not fall for flattery (Adcock). In this situation, guard against flattery and avoid people who do not seem genuine.

### Fifth line up

If you have this as a transforming line, you need to be sincere in all you do. At this point, being underhanded or deceitful in any way will damage your cause. Honesty and joyfulness should be your watchwords. Find the "blessed path" and follow it (Gill). Heaven will protect you if you stick to the correct way (Adcock). Look for the best person to follow (Huang). In this situation, look for the most moral way to progress; if you try to cheat your way through this you will come out the worse for it.

### Top line

If you have this as a transforming line, set clear parameters and objectives. Break down all the different parts of the challenge and ask yourself whether you can achieve them while remaining true to yourself. If you are working with others, make sure everyone knows their responsibilities and give them guidelines. Clarity is paramount. Listen out for great advice from others, but do not fall for lies (Adcock). In this situation, reassess your goal and map it out clearly.

## HEXAGRAM 18

**This hexagram represents: moving on and stopping the rot**

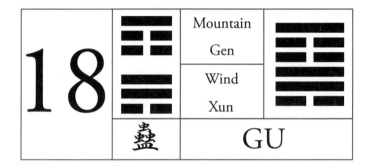

| | | Mountain | |
|---|---|---|---|
| 18 | | Gen | |
| | | Wind | |
| | | Xun | |
| | 蠱 | | GU |

READ ME FIRST

This hexagram appearing in your casting indicates that now is the proper time to attend to a stagnant situation. Consider which aspects of your life or situation are in decline or are decaying and what you can do to make a fresh start. The lower trigram is **Wind** and the upper trigram is **Mountain**. Commentators have interpreted this differently: some see it as the wind branching out around the mountain; others as the wind emerging from a valley. However, both images imply a change of direction. According to Huang, the **Mountain** trigram, representing the youngest son, and the **Wind** trigram, representing the eldest daughter, cancel each other out. This is because the eldest daughter is senior in age but the youngest son is senior in social standing (in the context of ancient Chinese culture, that is). In this situation there is a standstill and, therefore, a change in movement needs to take place. This hexagram can actually be represented by two different ideograms. One is of bamboo branching out, while the other is of rotting food and worms in an old jar. They seem completely different but they have similar connotations – of getting rid of decay, moving on and making a change.

**If you do not have any transforming lines:** find ways to eliminate negative aspects in your life without upsetting people or causing further issues. Avoid blaming others for what is not working in your life. Move on but leave people feeling happy. Avoid interacting with obviously hostile or negative people. Be aware that clinging to the past will decay your mind.

**If you do have transforming lines:** consult those lines within this hexagram for a more direct answer. Then transform your hexagram and focus just on the **Read me first** section of the new hexagram to discover what you should do.

### Bottom line
If you have this as a transforming line, root out any corruption within your life or your mind. You may have picked up a negative trait from those around you (Adcock). If someone else has left a mess for you to clean up, then it is best that you do it (Crisp). In this situation, do whatever has to be done to sort out the problem; do not complain, just deal with it.

### Second line up
If you have this as a transforming line, it is time to identify anything in your situation that needs to be thrown out. This could be people, influences, habits and so on. It is time to declutter your life, relationships and mind. However, be careful not to make enemies of the people you are leaving behind. It does not matter who is responsible for the problem, you just have to put it right (Adcock). There is no point dwelling on past mistakes (Huang). In this situation, fix what needs to be fixed without recriminations, but make sure that you do not leave an even bigger mess for someone else to clear up.

### Third line up
If you have this as a transforming line, do not dwell on any negative feelings you may have about a situation. If your intentions were pure, there is nothing to feel guilty about. It is best just to get on with sorting the problem out (Adcock). In this situation, let go of negative emotions and stop clinging to the past and the situation will resolve itself.

### Fourth line up

If you have this as a transforming line, monitor your situation closely. Some people may not be reliable, so investigate thoroughly before putting your trust in anyone. Deal with any problems you discover quickly but sensitively. If you let them fester they will grow (Adcock), so address the causes of the problems not the symptoms (Huang). In this situation, identify troublemakers and get rid of them without delay.

### Fifth line up

If you have this as a transforming line, it is time to prove your trustworthiness. Without being showy, display correct behaviour so people can clearly see that you are honest. Also, seek help from appropriate people (Huang). In this situation, demonstrate your merits but take care not to cause resentment.

### Top line

If you have this as a transforming line, realize that not all people will want to follow you or your ideas. If someone chooses a different path from yours, respect their decision. Equally, do not work for or follow anyone whose ideas do not fit with yours. If it means you have to travel your path alone do not be disheartened (Adcock). In this situation, stick to your principles but do not be upset if others want to take a different direction.

## HEXAGRAM 19

**This hexagram represents: arriving and approaching**

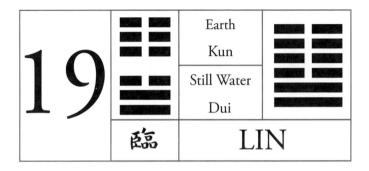

| 19 | ䷒ | Earth Kun | ䷒ |
| | | Still Water Dui | |
| | 臨 | LIN | |

### READ ME FIRST

This hexagram appearing in your casting warns of trouble ahead. The lower trigram is **Still Water** and the upper trigram is **Earth**. The image conveys the idea that those who stand on the land can see anything approaching across the lake. There may be an issue coming up in the future that you need to watch out for.

**If you do not have any transforming lines:** it is time to look out for anything coming your way, be it good or bad. Take care not to provoke people and prepare yourself for possible challenges. At the same time be open to new people and new situations.

**If you do have transforming lines:** consult those lines within this hexagram for a more direct answer. Then transform your hexagram and focus just on the **Read me first** section of the new hexagram to discover what you should do.

### Bottom line

If you have this as a transforming line, you will soon be recognized for your work or ideas. Prepare yourself for positive developments. However, stay disciplined and be wary. In this situation, look for opportunities that may arise and be ready to take them.

### Second line up

If you have this as a transforming line, set aside your doubts. What is troubling you will not develop into anything serious. Follow the righteous path and do what is correct in all things and you will get through any bad times to come (Adcock). Accept offers of help (Crisp), but beware of malicious characters (Huang). In this situation, be reassured that you are not in trouble or danger and let the right people in to help you.

### Third line up

If you have this as a transforming line, whatever your situation, make sure you are fully prepared. Check and recheck everything and wait for the next move. Keep your opinions and emotions to yourself so as not to annoy people (Adcock). If you have upset someone make your peace with them (Crisp). Reflect deeply on what has gone wrong in the past to anticipate what could go wrong in the future (Gill). In this situation, preparation is key; wait for an opening and make your move, but do not anger anyone.

### Fourth line up

If you have this as a transforming line, expect some kind of recognition for your work. People are noticing what you are doing or what you are aiming for. Also, stay open-minded about all people and all situations (Adcock), and keep going the way you are going because it is the correct way (Gill). In this situation, look to see whether anyone is paying you special attention; you may have overlooked someone who you did not expect to be interested in what you are doing.

### Fifth line up

If you have this as a transforming line, now is a time to act politely and sensitively. Do not be crass, brash or outspoken. Let the people who are here to help you do what they do best (Crisp). In this situation, treat people with respect and consideration and do not get in their way.

### Top line

If you have this as a transforming line, it is a time to be respectful and compassionate toward all of your friends and associates. Be very careful how you interact with other people; it may be that someone is on the verge of becoming upset. Use your personality to help people in need (Adcock). Also, find a teacher who can guide you (Crisp). In this situation, be on the alert for people around you who need your help.

## HEXAGRAM 20

**This hexagram represents: observing, watching and contemplation**

| 20 | Wind Xun | |
| | Earth Kun | |
| 觀 | GUAN | |

READ ME FIRST

This hexagram appearing in your casting means you should take time to observe a situation and consider if the move you are considering will really benefit you. The lower trigram is **Earth** and the upper trigram is **Wind**. The idea behind this image is that the wind moves over the land and sees everything.

**If you do not have any transforming lines:** look for what is best for you, but understand the difference between the things you want and the things you need. The thing you want may not benefit you ultimately, whereas the thing the universe knows you need may not be to your liking. It is time to take a broader view of the situation. Look at all angles and try to unshackle yourself from personal bias. Examine your mind to make sure it is being honest with you. This is a time to sit and think things through.

**If you do have transforming lines:** consult those lines within this hexagram for a more direct answer. Then transform your hexagram and focus just on the **Read me first** section of the new hexagram to discover what you should do.

## Bottom line

If you have this as a transforming line, try to observe the situation with an innocent and childlike mind. Release yourself from all the restrictions of adult thinking. Probe deeply to find your true thoughts on the matter. Alternatively, be careful not to lower your standards (Gill) or force others to follow you (Adcock) and be conscious of your own short-sightedness (Huang). In this situation, set aside your preconceptions and be honest with yourself.

## Second line up

If you have this as a transforming line, weigh up the strengths and weaknesses of who or what you are planning to follow. Why do you want to attach yourself to this group or this idea? Your view of the situation may be twisted; check your intention and only move forward in small increments (Gill). It is better to have a broad view than a narrow one (Huang) so make sure to get out and engage with the issues (Crisp). In this situation, observe where the real power is and question your motives – doing so might change the way you see your circumstances.

### Third line up

If you have this as a transforming line, be careful about what you are about to do. Ask yourself whether you are the right person to venture down this path. Look to your past for an example of what worked before (Gill) and manage both your own attitude and that of those under your control so that no one is insulted (Adcock). Do not follow people blindly; observe them first (Huang). In this situation, be aware that you may not be the best person for the task in question, but if you do decide to go down this path do so with a clear plan based on past successes.

### Fourth line up

If you have this as a transforming line, observe the people who are directly involved with the situation. The way they behave will help you decide what to do. If they conduct themselves dishonourably do not progress down this path; but if they are honest and good then you can proceed. Look above all at the most senior person involved. In this situation, avoid allying yourself with bad people; it will only change you.

### Fifth line up

If you have this as a transforming line, it is time that you adjusted your life to make an example to others of how they should run their lives. Show other people the righteous way, as long as you do truly follow that path. When you make a move or change, make sure it does not have a negative impact on other people (Gill). Also, believe in the people around you; they will help you (Adcock). Observe how people respond to you and if their reactions are negative consider whether you are doing something wrong (Huang). In this situation, set a good example and avoid doing anything that will cause anyone trouble.

### Top line

If you have this as a transforming line, start to look at the situation from other people's perspective. Compare their way of handling the situation to yours. Even if things are changing fast, still take time to think (Gill). Ask yourself whether any self-reflection in the past has made you change how you went about things or whether you just kept on in the same way (Adcock). Always remember that no matter how far you retreat from a situation, people will still observe you and make their own judgements on your behaviour (Huang). In this situation, try to see yourself as others see you and consider whether you are doing the right thing.

## HEXAGRAM 21

**This hexagram represents: progress and eradication**

| 21 | Fire Li / Thunder Zhen | |
|---|---|---|
| 噬嗑 | SHI HE | |

### READ ME FIRST

This hexagram appearing in your casting means that you should establish clear rules, guidelines and understandings before moving on. The lower hexagram is **Thunder** and the upper hexagram is **Fire**. The image is of bright fire and powerful thunder combining to suggest enlightened and strong judgement of a situation. The original Chinese revolves around the gnawing and chewing of meat, which implies progression through an issue. To "gnaw" on a problem or to "bite off more than you can chew" are examples of this imagery. Huang says that this is about biting through a problem, while Pearson states that the imagery in the original Chinese ideogram – which relates to punishment – is about what other people may do to you. According to this interpretation, the hexagram is warning you to be wary of those around you, but also to be fair. Adcock interprets the hexagram as there being a large piece of food in your mouth that needs to be chewed, meaning that there is something in the way of your goal that you need to find and remove in the most morally correct way. Gill says that in this situation there is a tough solution which needs to be enforced.

**If you do not have any transforming lines:** eradicate any negative aspects in the situation. You need to stay strong no matter what but always be fair. This may be a time where you have to act even if you do not want to, but keep out of trouble. Your main task is to get rid of a problem that is in your way.

**If you do have transforming lines:** consult those lines within this hexagram for a more direct answer. Then transform your hexagram and focus just on the **Read me first** section of the new hexagram to discover what you should do.

### Bottom line
If you have this as a transforming line, it means that you should not be too hard on whoever has caused a problem, whether it be yourself or someone else. Let it go. The more you worry and fuss about the problem, the bigger it becomes. In this situation, do not hold on to anger or regret; accept what has happened and move on.

### Second line up
If you have this as a transforming line, it means that you should punish appropriately any mistakes that have been made. Be direct, honest and straight and, above all, be fair. Do not worry if you have gone too far, but try to resolve any problems you have caused. In this situation, carefully measure your response to all misdeeds; do not be too harsh or too lenient.

### Third line up
If you have this as a transforming line, be firm and hard with someone who has done you wrong, or even with yourself if it is you who is to blame. Any problems must be resolved. Be strict but fair. This might not be easy for you, but make sure you do it. Alternatively, step back from the problem (Adcock). In this situation, you may have to treat someone more severely than you are used to.

### Fourth line up
If you have this as a transforming line, it means you are morally correct in this situation. Find a higher power or authority to back you up and keep going with your original idea or decision. Stay firm like a "golden shaft", maintaining your unbendable resolve. Keep your internal balance

(Adcock), always remain honest (Gill) and be careful of other people's jealousy (Crisp). In this situation you should stand your ground, seek people who will help you stay firm and do not be swayed by any problems.

### Fifth line up

If you have this as a transforming line, be wary of deviousness in the people around you. Someone may be treating you unfairly and twisting the situation in their favour. Something is not right. Find the issue but do not overreact. Remain impartial in any judgements you make (Adcock). In this situation, guard against people who wish you ill, but do not retaliate; simply standing clear of the issue will neutralize it.

### Top line

If you have this as a transforming line, consider giving people the benefit of the doubt. There may be someone who has set themselves against you, but do not take this to heart. Deal with the situation fairly and do not hold a grudge. If you push things too far in any direction it will cause you trouble (Adcock). Even so, do not ignore the situation or you will continue to be wronged (Gill). This cannot be allowed to happen. In this situation, forgive people who have done you wrong but make sure it does not happen again.

## HEXAGRAM 22

**This hexagram represents: adornment, elegance and grace**

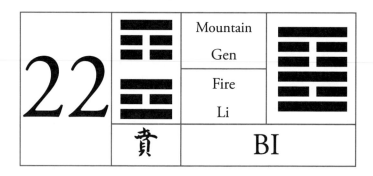

| 22 | Mountain Gen | |
| | Fire Li | |
| | 賁 | BI |

This hexagram appearing in your casting means that you should take a new look at your surroundings. Brighten things up, add some decoration, get around to making long-needed repairs or improvements. The lower trigram is **Fire** and the upper trigram is **Mountain**. The image is of flames illuminating and decorating the slopes of the mountain, making it glow with beauty in the night. Alternatively, Crisp says that a fire within your foundations creates an illuminated spirit.

**If you do not have any transforming lines:** be aware that sometimes you need to focus on the image the world sees, and sometimes you need to focus on your inner self. Understand the difference between what people present as a truth and what is actually true. Remember, an ordered room is the product of an ordered mind, so keep both your emotions and surroundings simple but elegant. It does not have to be a complete makeover; small improvements can work wonders.

**If you do have transforming lines:** consult those lines within this hexagram for a more direct answer. Then transform your hexagram and focus just on the **Read me first** section of the new hexagram to discover what you should do.

### Bottom line
If you have this as a transforming line, it implies that you need to step up your efforts. The original says to "clothe the feet and get out of the carriage", meaning walk instead of travel in luxury. Be modest in whatever you do (Adcock). In this situation, stop taking the easy way and put the effort in; if you want to get what you want, you need to work for it.

### Second line up
If you have this as a transforming line, it is time to smarten up. Something is not correct in how you appear to the outside world. Improve your image but also make sure there is a good person behind the façade (Gill). Learn how to look through the external images people project and perceive their true selves (Adcock). In this situation, focus on how you look but understand the difference between someone's appearance and their essence.

### Third line up

If you have this as a transforming line, it means that something needs changing within yourself. Do not focus on how you present yourself to the world, focus on how to correct your thinking and behaviour. If your life is going well then do not let it change your personality. If you have talent remember that you also need the drive to make the most of it (Gill). Do not fall into complacency (Adcock). In this situation, forget how you look to other people; sort your mind out first.

### Fourth line up

If you have this as a transforming line, do not hide or distort the truth by using sophisticated language. Be honest in what you say and honest in how you deal with a situation. If you "adorn" the air with your words it will end badly for you. Have no stains on your character and be pure inside. Avoid showing off or trying to impress people (Adcock). In this situation, speak and act plainly and honestly.

### Fifth line up

If you have this as a transforming line, be careful about your resources at this point. Do not spend a great deal of money, time or effort on something that will not be worth it. Spend what you have to (Gill), but treasure above all else your own inner nature (Huang). Alternatively, do not take sides (Adcock). In this situation, focus your resources on that which is essential to your cause.

### Top line

If you have this as a transforming line, it is time to simplify your mind, your persona, your surroundings or anything else which is becoming too complex. Avoid unnecessary things and stay true to your beliefs. Find beauty in simplicity (Gill). If you keep pushing too hard you will fail (Adcock). In this situation, cut back on things you do not need; minimalism not excess is what will get you to the next stage.

# HEXAGRAM 23

**This hexagram represents: decline, peeling back and falling away**

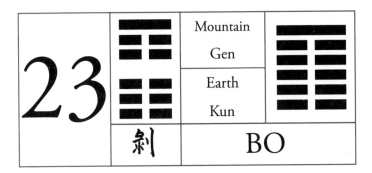

| 23 | Mountain Gen / Earth Kun | |
|---|---|---|
| 剝 | BO | |

**READ ME FIRST**

This hexagram appearing in your casting means that you have to shed something from your life to make progress. The lower trigram is **Earth** and the upper trigram is **Mountain**. It conveys the idea that, just as a mountain is supported by the earth, nothing reaches high without solid foundations.

**If you do not have any transforming lines:** something in your situation is rotten, declining or falling apart and it needs to be removed. This could be a way of thinking or behaving or an attachment to something or someone. If you try to push forward now you will not get far until your dead weight has been cut loose. Stand for what is correct and do not give in, but overall detach yourself from negativity or unrealistic situations.

**If you do have transforming lines:** consult those lines within this hexagram for a more direct answer. Then transform your hexagram and focus just on the **Read me first** section of the new hexagram to discover what you should do.

## Bottom line

If you have this as a transforming line, look at the foundations of the situation. It is as if you have a piece of furniture and paint is peeling off from the bottom because moisture is getting in. Something or someone within the situation you are in needs your attention. Therefore, keep everything that supports you in good repair, even down to the person or thing that is at the very bottom. Swiftly remove any threats to your ideas (Gill). In this situation, deal with any damage, however minor it may seem.

## Second line up

If you have this as a transforming line, look to those who support you and make sure that they are well taken care of. The damage to your piece of furniture (see bottom line for this hexagram) is spreading; the paint is now peeling off all the way up the legs and almost to the halfway mark. Be sure to check everyone and everything that is helping you at this point. Something you have overlooked may be causing internal damage. Maybe if you switch position it will help you see what the problems are (Crisp). Alternatively, if you show your intentions to people around you who are evil they may use it against you (Gill), so do not get too deeply involved with the problem (Adcock). In this situation, you need to address a problem that is corrupting your ideas from the inside.

## Third line up

If you have this as a transforming line, it means there is no way to fix the problems that are affecting you at this time. It is best to have a clean break and move on to something new (Crisp). If you get more involved it will cause you problems, but if you extract yourself from the situation there is no way people can honestly blame you (Gill). Stay on the true path. In this situation, detach yourself from a problematic situation and start again.

## Fourth line up

If you have this as a transforming line, it means the rot has set in so much that there is no point trying to fix the problem. Your whole situation is riddled with rot and crumbling away. It is time to move on or you will encounter serious difficulties. Try to find help (Crisp), because the situation is not great for you (Gill). Alternatively, endure this bad situation and wait for things to calm down (Adcock). In this situation, accept that the damage is irreversible and it is definitely time to start anew.

## Fifth line up

If you have this as a transforming line, you need to get out of the clutches of someone or something that is looking to bring you down. Retreat to a safer place. The brighter your soul shines the harder it is for evil to get close to you (Huang). People follow you because of your true nature (Gill). Seek help from other people (Crisp). If you accept the situation as it is, things will get better (Adcock). In this situation, get yourself to a place you can defend and you will not be defeated.

## Top line

If you have this as a transforming line, know that if you have stripped away all corruption, both within and around you, people will follow you faithfully. Those who stand by their beliefs and shun negativity are inspiring to others. Allow your inner light to chase away the threats that hide in the shadows. Now is a time to look to the future (Adcock). In this situation, show people your determination to fight for what is true.

# HEXAGRAM 24

**This hexagram represents: returning, starting again and turning back**

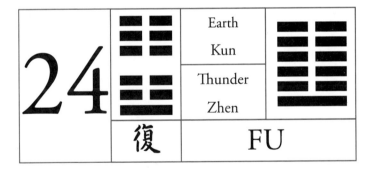

| 24 | Earth<br>Kun | |
| | Thunder<br>Zhen | |
| | 復 | FU |

READ ME FIRST

This hexagram appearing in your casting means that if you are in difficulty then it should not be long before things right themselves. The lower trigram is **Thunder** and the upper trigram is **Earth**. The image is one of an earthquake, which changes everything for a short period but then subsides, allowing life to return to normal.

**If you do not have any transforming lines:** you need to get back to a better position. This could mean, for example, recovering your former strength, correcting a harmful mistake you have made or restoring a happy state of affairs. In short, your task right now is not to gain something new but to retrieve what you have lost.

**If you do have transforming lines:** consult those lines within this hexagram for a more direct answer. Then transform your hexagram and focus just on the **Read me first** section of the new hexagram to discover what you should do.

### Bottom line

If you have this as a transforming line, it means you have to correct something straight away. Retrace your steps and fix any errors. The longer you leave it, the more harm will be done. Make a fresh start for better fortune. In this situation, correct the problem now or regret it later.

### Second line up

If you have this as a transforming line, take a break before making your next move. Settle down and relax. Do not push forward. Instead gather yourself for a while until it is time to move on again. This may be a time to learn from other people (Adcock). In this situation, you will make a mistake if you rush ahead; stop, think and observe.

### Third line up

If you have this as a transforming line, keep trying no matter how many times it takes before you get it right. However, if you continue to fail in your objective ask yourself whether what you are doing is actually correct. Alternatively, returning to the original position may be the wrong thing to do (Gill). Do not constantly change your mind (Crisp) and do not fixate on bad habits (Adcock). In this situation, if you keep trying something and it is not working ask yourself honestly whether this is the right thing for you to be doing; if you still believe it is, then take yourself back to square one and go for it again.

### Fourth line up

If you have this as a transforming line, do not be swayed by popular ideas. The thing that the majority believes is not necessarily correct. Good friends will not mind if you disagree with them (Adcock). In this situation, follow your instincts not the crowd.

### Fifth line up

If you have this as a transforming line, admit to any mistakes you may have made. Look to make amends and correct your actions. If you are called upon to justify what you are doing, do not assume that you are in the right (Adcock). In this situation, ask yourself whether what you are doing is correct before you continue doing it.

### Top line

If you have this as a transforming line, it means that you have made a mistake somewhere along the line and you need to rectify it or there will be massive problems to face. Be very careful. In this situation, go back over everything you have done and everyone you have interacted with, find the problem and fix it.

## HEXAGRAM 25

**This hexagram represents: being wronged, blamelessness and innocence**

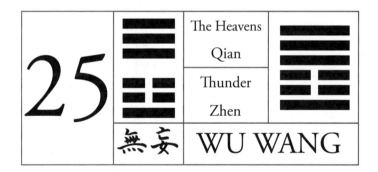

| 25 | | The Heavens | |
| | | Qian | |
| | | Thunder | |
| | | Zhen | |
| 無妄 | WU WANG | | |

READ ME FIRST

This hexagram appearing in your casting means that there may be something or someone who is causing a problem in the situation you are enquiring about. The lower trigram is **Thunder** and the upper trigram is **The Heavens**, implying thunder and darkness across the sky. It is a time to be alert to any malign influences directed toward you. The original Chinese for this hexagram means "to be without falsehood". The idea is of an innocent person being a victim of aggression or lies.

**If you do not have any transforming lines:** you need to stand still, do not let negative feelings eat away at you and wait for the darkness to pass over you. It is as if you are being blamed for someone else's crime. But stand fast, truth will out in the end. Stay clear of any problems, now is not the time to get involved.

**If you do have transforming lines:** consult those lines within this hexagram for a more direct answer. Then transform your hexagram and focus just on the **Read me first** section of the new hexagram to discover what you should do.

### Bottom line
If you have this as a transforming line, it means that what you are doing is correct. Trust your gut feeling (Adcock); move out and forward to achieve what you want (Gill). In this situation, things may seem dark but no one can stand in the way of your plans, so press on.

### Second line up
If you have this as a transforming line, it means you have to put the work in before you can expect rewards. Remind yourself how you reached this point. Daydreaming will get you nowhere (Gill). In this situation, wake up, ask yourself how you got into this position and then do something about it.

### Third line up
If you have this as a transforming line, be careful of people making false accusations against you. Does someone want to make you the scapegoat or are circumstances putting you in a vulnerable position? Hold fast and ride through this difficult situation or, better still, avoid it if you can. Sometimes you have to accept that bad things happen to good people (Crisp). In this situation, take misfortune or mistreatment on the chin and move on.

### Fourth line up
If you have this as a transforming line, keep your head held high and continue to behave correctly even toward people who are saying malicious things about you. Do not let other people persuade you to take the wrong path (Adcock). Make sure that you remain honest throughout this time

(Gill). In this situation, do not rise to provocation or get involved in something you should not be doing.

### Fifth line up

If you have this as a transforming line, it means you may be in a difficult situation now. Do not fight against the situation, or anyone who is directing hate toward you. Stick to the correct path and their efforts will fade away leaving you in a better position. Things will pass by their own accord so just wait (Gill). In this situation, restrain yourself; the situation will change for the better.

### Top line

If you have this as a transforming line, do not make a move at this point. If you get involved in something now you will become entangled in problems. Make sure the time is exactly right for you to do anything (Huang). In this situation, wait for a better opportunity; the time is not right.

## HEXAGRAM 26

**This hexagram represents: gaining, increasing and accumulating power**

| 26 | Mountain Gen | |
| | The Heavens Qian | |
| 大畜 | DA CHU | |

READ ME FIRST

This hexagram appearing in your casting means your power is building or at its height. The lower trigram is **The Heavens** and the upper trigram is **Mountain**. Imagine yourself standing on a mountain peak looking down on the clouds as they accumulate and prepare to release their precious rain. Huang says that this hexagram represents a time of great potential and it is for you to decide whether to unleash that potential or hold it back. All interpretations put you in a position of strength; it is just a question of when you use it.

**If you do not have any transforming lines:** rethink what you are going to do and avoid stepping into people's traps. Use your head not your heart. If you are going to go forward now, do it with all your effort. If you decide to wait, do so for the right reasons. If your inaction is through laziness or procrastination, you may be missing a vital opportunity.

**If you do have transforming lines:** consult those lines within this hexagram for a more direct answer. Then transform your hexagram and focus just on the **Read me first** section of the new hexagram to discover what you should do.

### Bottom line

If you have this as a transforming line, pause for a final check before you act. Go back through everything you know to help you see the situation from all angles. Moving too early could cause a problem. In this situation, stop and check. If you still think it is a good idea, go for it.

### Second line up

If you have this as a transforming line, understand that there are two directly opposing interpretations. Some translators see the line as representing a vehicle with the brakes released and so they say that you should not wait – now is the time to engage with the situation fully (Moran). To others the line represents a vehicle with a broken part and so they say that it would be dangerous to make a move now (Huang, Gill and Crisp). In this situation, as the I-Ching community cannot agree on what this line means, look at what is going on around you and think deeply. You should either act now or wait. Go with your instincts.

### Third line up

If you have this as a transforming line, move into action and do not let up in your efforts. You have made the decision, so put everything you have into it. However, keep checking as you go and look out for trouble (Crisp). In this situation, either act with all your heart or do not act at all.

### Fourth line up

If you have this as a transforming line, pay attention to small details. Make sure everything is in the right place and check your facts and figures. Only when everything adds up should you move into action. Make sure the way is safe before you set off (Huang). Stop any problems from arising before they start (Crisp) and do not let your emotions get the better of you. In this situation, use your head not your heart to prepare for action.

### Fifth line up

If you have this as a transforming line, ignore any bad things that people may be saying about you. Stay well clear of people who are jealous of you. Focus on the positives, not the negatives. If someone is acting against your cause, use tactics to nullify their attack (Huang). Stay calm in the face of provocation (Crisp). By not reacting in the way your opponents want you to react, you take away their power. In this situation, do not surrender your power to these people by giving them your attention.

### Top line

If you have this as a transforming line, it means your aims are supported by the universe. What you are doing is righteous. In this situation, it is time to unleash your ideas.

## HEXAGRAM 27

**This hexagram represents: physical and spiritual nourishment**

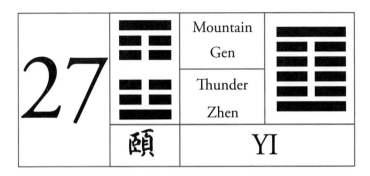

| 27 | | Mountain Gen | |
| | | Thunder Zhen | |
| | 頤 | YI | |

READ ME FIRST

This hexagram appearing in your casting means you have to be mindful of the purity of both your mind and body. The lower trigram is **Thunder** and the upper trigram is **Mountain**. The image is of thunder moving about the mountain, just as the lower jaw moves and the upper jaw is still when chewing food. The original Chinese used for this hexagram is "jaws" and implies that the food that you chew nourishes your body and, by extension, your health. On all levels, think of nourishing your mind and your body for a better life.

**If you do not have any transforming lines:** think about nourishing yourself and nourishing others. To work on your inner ideas, and your physical body if it needs it, do not just go for the easy option. The difficult path will take you to a healthier reward. Avoid letting people steer you into situations that will not lead you to become a better person.

**If you do have transforming lines:** consult those lines within this hexagram for a more direct answer. Then transform your hexagram and focus just on the **Read me first** section of the new hexagram to discover what you should do.

### Bottom line

If you have this as a transforming line, do not distract yourself by comparing your situation to that of others. Envy will get you nowhere. You have your own life and your own tests. You have all you need at the moment (Adcock). In this situation, shut out the rest of the world and work on yourself.

### Second line up

If you have this as a transforming line, make sure you help the right people. Sometimes it is best to help those who really need it and not those who will be of benefit to you. Further still, sometimes it is better to be independent (Huang). Do not look to others to make you strong at this time (Adcock); you have the magic inside you (Crisp) so go with that. In this situation, work on yourself, and help people who are in real need not the people you think will be able to help you in return.

### Third line up

If you have this as a transforming line, be careful about who you connect with. It is tempting to connect with people who will help you the most: the most powerful, the most beautiful, and so on. But this might be a mistake at this point in your life. Consider why you are engaging with each person; if it is not for the right reasons, find more appropriate people to connect with instead. If you keep doing the wrong thing it may be years before you recover your position (Gill). Attaching yourself to desires is a waste of time (Adcock). Do not pursue physical or mental pleasures that will ruin you (Crisp). In this situation, find the hard road and follow it; the easy option is not always good for you.

### Fourth line up

If you have this as a transforming line, beware of people trying to manipulate you into doing something you know is wrong. Do not give favours which are not deserved and do not twist the rules even if they are making life difficult for you. Stick to your principles. It may even be good to withdraw from the issue for a while (Gill). In this situation, do not fall for dodgy schemes; people who want to bring you down or leech off you should not be allowed to do so.

### Fifth line up

If you have this as a transforming line, it is a time to wait. Your ideas or actions might not be in line with everyone else's, but you are right to stick to your principles. Do not force any issues at this time. If you do make a move, commit to it fully (Huang). Now is a time to be vigilant about what you absorb, both into your stomach and into your mind – it may not be good for you (Gill). Focus on perfecting your mind and body before helping others (Adcock) and do not invest too much in an issue if you are not sure about it (Crisp). In this situation, remain pure, patient and positive.

### Top line

If you have this as a transforming line, it means that any actions you have taken in the past have done their work and have created the situation you are in. This is a positive thing if you are in a positive place. Now move into action. Be aware, if you are not already, that you are a significant figure in other people's lives (Gill). Remain humble, even if others elevate you

(Adcock). In this situation, fulfil what you have set out to do because the things you need are in place if you can find them.

## HEXAGRAM 28

**This hexagram represents: a testing time, surpassing and exceeding**

| 28 | | Still Water Dui | |
| | | Wind Xun | |
| | 大過 | DA GUO | |

### READ ME FIRST

This hexagram appearing in your casting means that you are in a testing situation that must be overcome. It is as if there is too much weight on the roof of your house and the beams are ready to break. The lower trigram is **Wind** (or, in this case, **Wood**) and the upper trigram is **Still Water**. The image is of a flood rising through a forest. Right now, the situation is dangerous but in the end the water will drain away.

**If you do not have any transforming lines:** there is an external force putting pressure on you and you have to resist it. One way to do this is by pushing back directly; another way is to retreat from the pressure. Above all, keep control of the situation. Remember that sometimes engaging with a problem causes it to escalate, so it may be better to stand off.

**If you do have transforming lines:** consult those lines within this hexagram for a more direct answer. Then transform your hexagram and focus just on the **Read me first** section of the new hexagram to discover what you should do.

### Bottom line

If you have this as a transforming line, it is time to show others that you are there to help with a true heart. Be careful in all you do and act with a gentle character. Retreating at this point might be a good idea (Adcock). Address any weaknesses in your position (Gill). In this situation, offer genuine help to other people and approach them in a non-threatening way.

### Second line up

If you have this as a transforming line, it is best not to overreact, whatever the situation. When a tree is chopped back, it puts all its energy into sending out new shoots or suckers. Be aware of people trying to take control from you and sap your energy. It is time to balance the situation; make sure that everything is in order and that nothing is dragging you down (Huang). Go forward slowly and with care (Adcock). In this situation, keep things in perspective and in order, and stay in control of the issue.

### Third line up

If you have this as a transforming line, there is a considerable possibility that someone or something is set against you, so be particularly vigilant. Do not allow people through your defences too easily. Alternatively, do not be too strict or rigid in your attitude; allow for some flexibility (Huang). Avoid immersing yourself in desire (Adcock). Listen to the advice of others, because if you carry on regardless things will go badly (Crisp). In this situation, watch out for people trying to get one over on you; and keep control without being overbearing.

### Fourth line up

If you have this as a transforming line, the problem you are facing is one that you can easily fix. Do not let it bother you too much, but make sure you actually do something about it. Alternatively, do not abuse people's trust (Adcock). Look to those who will help you in earnest (Crisp). While the situation is bad, it can be remedied (Gill). In this situation, ease yourself out of any problems and earn people's faith in you.

### Fifth line up

If you have this as a transforming line, know that any actions you take may fix the problem you are facing but they will not bring you great rewards or acclamation. It is not that tackling the situation head on is bad, but it will not push you forward. Either deal with it or put it to one side, but do not make a fuss of it. Consider looking for someone wise to help you (Adcock). In this situation, solving a problem may be a thankless task.

### Top line

If you have this as a transforming line, now is the time to persevere without fear of your opposition and to endure any situation with an iron heart. You are in deep water so do not keep pushing forward but be patient (Adcock). In this situation, maintain your resolve to your very core.

## HEXAGRAM 29

**This hexagram represents: dangerous situations, deep problems and darkness**

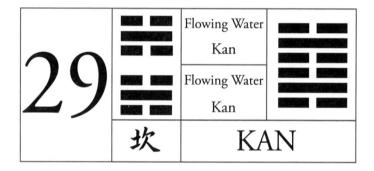

| 29 | Flowing Water Kan | |
|----|-------------------|--|
|    | Flowing Water Kan | |
| 坎 | KAN | |

READ ME FIRST

This hexagram appearing in your casting means the situation you are in could turn into a really big problem, so you need to be careful or you will be in dire straits. The lower and upper trigrams are both **Flowing Water**. The image is of fast flowing water within the landscape, which often falls into gorges or sink holes and deep dark places. This is a very negative and dangerous image.

**If you do not have any transforming lines:** you may have to wait before you take action. Do not underestimate the seriousness of the situation you are in. The original characters mean a great and deep abyss, which does not bode well. This is a time to take great care in what you do to avoid great misfortune, but also consider how to deal with weighty problems. If you have to carry on in this situation, be on guard, tread with care and ask yourself whether you are responsible for things being so bad.

**If you do have transforming lines:** consult those lines within this hexagram for a more direct answer. Then transform your hexagram and focus just on the **Read me first** section of the new hexagram to discover what you should do.

## Bottom line
If you have this as a transforming line, do not struggle too much in your situation. You may have to wait it out. No matter how difficult things get, believe in yourself (Huang) and make sure to look out for any danger that is facing you (Adcock). Consider asking for help if needs be (Crisp). In this situation, do not take any risks.

## Second line up
If you have this as a transforming line, do not overreact to anything. Take small steps and push through, but do so with much planning and double checking. Go slow and with care and give yourself time to gain new energy (Gill). Do all you can to see your way through this situation (Crisp). In this situation, be fully on guard and do nothing hasty.

## Third line up
If you have this as a transforming line, there is more danger around you than you think. Now is the time to go fully on the defensive and hide out in a safe place for a while, be it in your mind, in a relationship or in purely physical terms. Do not struggle against the flow which is around you now. If you do it will overcome you because it is too strong, so wait for your time to move (Huang). Find a still place to wait and ride out the problems (Adcock). In this situation, there is danger all around you, so prioritize protection over movement.

## Fourth line up
If you have this as a transforming line, simplify your situation, your life and your thoughts. Extravagant, excessive or overbearing behaviour will cause you problems. Now is the time to be frugal and minimalistic in your mind, body and relationships with other people. Let any problems pass by

and be sincere and faithful in your interactions (Huang). Also, it is good to seek help in this situation (Gill). Be thankful for anything good at the moment and value what you have (Crisp). In this situation, keep things simple and stay alert.

## Fifth line up

If you have this as a transforming line, the situation you are in is a problem but it should not get worse. Stay level-headed and keep faith in yourself and the path you have chosen and you will get through. Things come in their correct time, so now is a time to go with the flow (Adcock). Stay alert, the danger is there but it is not getting worse (Gill). If you can just keep your head above water, you will get through this (Crisp). In this situation, hold tight and you will overcome this bad situation.

## Top line

If you have this as a transforming line, the problems you are facing go deep. It will take you a long time to resolve them, so prepare yourself for the long haul. Clear your mind of all negative thoughts and follow only the righteous way (Huang). Wrong thinking is clouding the true answer to your question (Adcock). In this situation, you are not in a good place; go deep inside yourself and ask why you want what you want or do what you do.

# HEXAGRAM 30

**This hexagram represents: brightness, cohesion and clinging together**

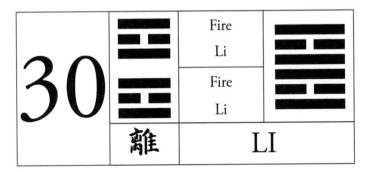

| | | Fire | |
| | | Li | |
| 30 | | Fire | |
| | | Li | |
| | 離 | LI | |

**READ ME FIRST**

This hexagram appearing in your casting means that you should "shine a light" on your thoughts and intentions. Bring things into the open and let people see what you are about and what you are doing. The lower and upper trigrams are both **Fire**. The overwhelming image that this conveys is brightness. Huang says that in times of darkness people bind together with others to produce a brightness around themselves. Pearson explains that the ancient Chinese use the character for "net" here, meaning "cohesion".

**If you do not have any transforming lines:** consider forming alliances with other people and working within a group. Now is the time for bonding with people around you but make sure you do so with grace. Avoid any people or activities that hinder you and drain your energy and time; instead focus on who or what can fundamentally help you.

**If you do have transforming lines:** consult those lines within this hexagram for a more direct answer. Then transform your hexagram and focus just on the **Read me first** section of the new hexagram to discover what you should do.

## Bottom line

If you have this as a transforming line, it means that if or when you seek help, ask people from any walk of life but do not allow them to confuse the situation or your aim. Make sure that everyone in the group clearly understands their role and your intentions. It may be that you are only at the start of the process and cannot see how things will end, so tread carefully (Huang). In this situation, look to others for help but remain clear and transparent at all times.

### Second line up

If you have this as a transforming line, you need to rely on honest people to help you out. If you are to attach yourself to something or someone, make sure it is the correct situation or the correct person (Huang). You need to act with moderation at this time (Adcock). In this situation, find people who are of true heart and do not push things too far.

### Third line up

If you have this as a transforming line, look at the people around you and work out who is not pulling their weight. Someone may be hampering your efforts because their rhythm is different from yours; make sure everyone is working in unison. Also, do not be sorrowful about anything; find whatever happiness the situation can offer. You must accept that things appear in their own time (Adcock). It is not good behaviour to lament that which must come to an end (Gill). In this situation, do not try to bend fate and be conscious of anyone who may be hindering you.

### Fourth line up

If you have this as a transforming line, be wary of anyone who seems to be very enthusiastic, or even over-enthusiastic. Their interest and energy will most likely soon run out and they will leave you where you started. Do not try to do too much too soon or you will burn yourself out; instead spread your energy over time. Deal with any surprises in a non-reactive way and stay true (Huang). Make sure to persevere through this time (Adcock). In this situation, avoid doing too much at once; ration your efforts but do not be lazy.

### Fifth line up

If you have this as a transforming line, look out for people who may have been hurt or had difficulties in the past. If you take care of these people they will become good allies. Likewise, heal your own pain from the past and be careful not to open old wounds. Remain humble at this time for a better future (Adcock). Show true repentance if it is needed (Gill). In this situation, heal wounds – both your own and those of other people.

## Top line

If you have this as a transforming line, look for the fundamental problem in your situation. If it seems that you are being opposed by many people or a great force look for the root cause of the conflict and resolve it through your own strength and effort, but do not try to solve any extraneous issues. Remove the key problem and all will be well. Also, consider that the problem you need to remove may lie within your own mind (Adcock). In this situation, all of your problems come from a single source; fix that issue and everything else will fall into place.

# 易經

# THE I-CHING:
# LOWER CANON

# THE I-CHING: LOWER CANON

The remaining 34 hexagrams of the I-Ching are often referred to as the Lower Canon and are considered to represent those things below the heavens, such as the earth and humans. In Chinese culture earthly aspects are associated with *yin* energy (see page 39). However, it should be remembered that in the original I-Ching the idea of *yinyang* theory had yet to be fully developed. It was later commentators who applied the distinction between *yin* and *yang* hexagrams.

## HEXAGRAM 31

**This hexagram represents: influence, attraction and reciprocity**

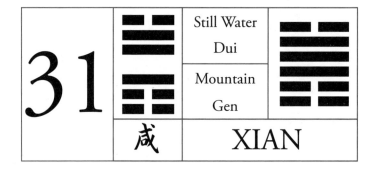

| 31 | ䷞ (Still Water / Dui, Mountain / Gen) | Still Water Dui | |
| | | Mountain Gen | |
| | 咸 | XIAN | |

**READ ME FIRST**

This hexagram appearing in your casting refers to relationships between people, influence and the joining together of different people or groups of people. The lower trigram is **Mountain** – or in this case the foot of the mountain – and the upper trigram is **Still Water**. The image is that the mountain replenishes the still water below it as rain runs down and finds the lowest level, and the water in the lake nourishes life at the foot of the mountain. So, each exerts an important influence on the other.

**If you do not have any transforming lines:** focus on the connections, whether good or bad, between yourself and the people around you. The answer to your question lies there. Look to the influences people have on you and those you have on others and consider if everything is as it should be. The whole situation you are in rests on how you deal with people and bring them together. Make sure you only deal with the correct people.

**If you do have transforming lines:** consult those lines within this hexagram for a more direct answer. Then transform your hexagram and focus just on the **Read me first** section of the new hexagram to discover what you should do.

### Bottom line

If you have this as a transforming line, look at the people involved within the situation you are enquiring about. Study how they lead their lives, the decisions they make and the way in which they behave. This will show you their true nature. At this stage, the situation has developed too little to determine where you should go (Huang), so make sure to keep things solid and clear (Adcock). In this situation, test others to see if they are correct for you and start to map out the best plan.

### Second line up

If you have this as a transforming line, be wary of someone who comes to you or is already within your situation who may have hidden intent to do you harm in some way. Be careful of anyone who approaches, making sure to curb your impulses (Gill). Things may take more time than you expect (Adcock). In this situation, save energy for the long haul and do not let the wrong people in.

### Third line up

If you have this as a transforming line, do not just accept the people around you now for who they are. Thoroughly examine all aspects of people or the situation; do not walk blindly into anything. You must have patience at this point (Huang). Do not use your influence for selfish means (Adcock) or follow your passions to a dark place (Crisp). If you rely too much on people you will not get good results (Gill). In this situation, take time to reflect – both on yourself and the people around you – and keep all your dealings honest and true.

## Fourth line up

If you have this as a transforming line, do not dwell on any past problems. Instead make a fresh start and set out in a clear direction. Make everything simple and straightforward. You must eliminate any selfish desires (Huang) and make sure to spread positivity to others at this time (Adcock) or you may lose people who support you (Gill). In this situation, if you become a dreary bore people may turn away from you; stay positive.

## Fifth line up

If you have this as a transforming line, it is time to reward, look after or take time to appreciate the people around you. Showing your love for others will help any changes you make go smoothly. Avoid those who only say sweet words but have no substance, and take proper time to evaluate the situation (Huang). Stay true to your ideas but allow for some flexibility (Adcock). In this situation, do not push too hard or talk too much; show kindness and love and do not let things get out of hand.

## Top line

If you have this as a transforming line, look at those around you and anyone directly involved in the situation you are in. Observe how they talk, how they look and how they hold themselves to understand more about how you should deal with them. Always keep your word (Huang) and back up everything you say (Crisp). It is time to make what you say a reality, so move to action (Adcock). In this situation, put your plans into effect, using people you trust, but only if you know you can do it or give it a serious attempt.

# HEXAGRAM 32

**This hexagram represents: consistency and durability**

| 32 | ䷟ | Thunder Zhen | ䷟ |
| | | Wind Xun | |
| | 恆 | HENG | |

**READ ME FIRST**

This hexagram appearing in your casting represents stability, continuation and loyalty. The lower trigram is **Wind** and the upper trigram is **Thunder**. The image is of thunder on the wind, its sound reverberating for miles around as it travels onward through the sky. Huang says that Thunder represents the oldest male child while Wind symbolizes the oldest female child (see pages 50–51), giving an image of a happy couple from two families who have a long future ahead of them. The implication is that you too should look to build a steady and ongoing future in the situation you are in.

**If you do not have any transforming lines:** at the moment the foundations of your situation are not stable enough. You need to focus on securing your position before moving on so that your situation, idea or goal will have longevity. Building strong bonds is worth spending time over, but building the wrong links will be devastating.

**If you do have transforming lines:** consult those lines within this hexagram for a more direct answer. Then transform your hexagram and focus just on the **Read me first** section of the new hexagram to discover what you should do.

**Bottom line**

If you have this as a transforming line, do not force a connection with someone. Make small steps to build a strong foundation for a great future with them. This person will be able to help you make a lot of progress but do not force them or it will not work out. In this situation, build strong bonds over time or risk collapse.

### Second line up
If you have this as a transforming line, let go of the past and start afresh. This may relate to a relationship with someone or a whole situation. Trying to build on damaged foundations will not get you anywhere. Stay on solid ground, find your feet and trust your inner voice (Adcock). The situation you are in will not last long if you do not have stability in your life (Gill). In this situation, building a solid foundation is essential.

### Third line up
If you have this as a transforming line, be careful not to establish a relationship with the wrong person. The person may appear to be positive, but have the wrong underlying attitude. Do not compare yourself to others, focus on yourself (Adcock) and reconnect with who you are and what you stand for (Crisp). If you are disloyal this will cause problems (Gill). In this situation, build bonds with the correct people, not those you *hope* are correct.

### Fourth line up
If you have this as a transforming line, it may be that you are putting time and effort into the wrong person or situation. Your overall goal may be correct but the current direction is bad. Like an empty hunting ground, there is no reward to be had here. Find a place or position that is beneficial to you (Huang) and maintain integrity (Adcock) because whatever is holding your attention now is not right for you at this moment (Crisp). In this situation, know the difference between what you want and what you need; it seems you have things the wrong way round.

### Fifth line up
If you have this as a transforming line, think deeply about which of your current relationships are worth pushing forward. It may be that some of your connections are dead in the water and should be abandoned. It is time to make tough decisions (Huang) but do not be too rigid (Adcock). In this situation, you have to come to terms with what is not working anymore and let it go.

### Top line

If you have this as a transforming line, look to any connections or relationships that are not working correctly. Ask yourself whether you should move on from them or keep trying. This is a risky move but search deep and come to an answer. Do what a sage would do and allow the universe to guide you (Adcock). Relax, step back and re-evaluate (Crisp). In this situation, find out what is working and what is not and cut away the dead wood.

## HEXAGRAM 33

**This hexagram represents: retiring and retreat**

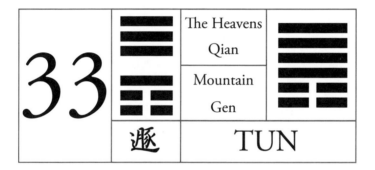

| 33 | ☰ | The Heavens Qian | |
| | ☶ | Mountain Gen | |
| | 遯 | TUN | |

**READ ME FIRST**

This hexagram appearing in your casting means that you should withdraw from the situation in question. The lower trigram is **Mountain** and the upper trigram is **The Heavens**. The image is either that you are blocked by a mountain which reaches up to the sky and you cannot go forward, or that you must retreat to the mountaintop and stay away from others for a while. Huang characterizes this as living like a sage following the way of heaven and being still like a mountain.

**If you do not have any transforming lines:** consider taking some time out of the situation to observe things from the outside, make new plans and come back to the issue at a later date. It might be best to step back before you cause trouble or do something you will regret.

**If you do have transforming lines:** consult those lines within this hexagram for a more direct answer. Then transform your hexagram and focus just on the **Read me first** section of the new hexagram to discover what you should do.

### Bottom line
If you have this as a transforming line, now is time to leave the situation. The sooner the better. But do not retreat so far that you become cut off (Gill). In this situation, stand back, do not get involved and wait for another time.

### Second line up
If you have this as a transforming line, it is best not to show favouritism to anyone or anything in the situation and then withdraw. Leave no one feeling malice toward you. Stay back for now, but always keep your goal in sight (Crisp). In this situation, let the opportunity pass or wait for a different time.

### Third line up
If you have this as a transforming line, avoid anyone or anything that is taking up too much of your time. Alternatively, help others to retreat from a situation (Gill); stay at home for the time being (Huang); or keep only trusted people around you (Crisp). In this situation, avoid getting involved in the issue at hand; instead help others who are in need, while making sure not to involve yourself in their problems.

### Fourth line up
If you have this as a transforming line, withdraw from the situation you are in, no matter how much regret this causes you. You would be a fool to stick around (Gill). Remove any negativity which clings to you (Huang); and try defusing problematic situations by releasing built-up pressure (Crisp). In this situation, ease back and let issues de-escalate.

### Fifth line up
If you have this as a transforming line, leave the situation you are in. This will help you clear your mind and focus on the correct action. Take a break from it all. Retreat in a controlled manner – do not just drop everything and run (Gill). If you cannot exit the situation fully then act with honesty,

otherwise problems will follow (Huang). Make sure that when you retreat from a situation you remain on good terms with people (Crisp). In this situation, try to make a clean exit but without upsetting people.

### Top line
If you have this as a transforming line, you must retreat to release the pressure from you and give you time to relax. If you keep going forward in this situation nothing good will come of it, but if you step back all will turn out well. In this situation, you would be a fool to carry on.

## HEXAGRAM 34

**This hexagram represents: strength and justified action**

| 34 | Thunder Zhen | |
|----|--------------|--|
|    | The Heavens Qian | |
| 大壯 | DA ZHUANG | |

READ ME FIRST

This hexagram appearing in your casting means that you should ask yourself whether the position you have built up is based on integrity and truth. If you can honestly say that it is, you are in a great situation. The lower trigram is **The Heavens** and the upper trigram is **Thunder**. The image is of the sky when thunder is roaring out. By this you know what true power means.

**If you do not have any transforming lines:** understand that the situation is about your power and whether you should use it or not. If you can justify the actions you are contemplating, then you should move forward but always be mindful of how that may anger others. Stand firm and be strong in your opinions and direction. Remember, as long as with your whole heart you can say you have not been deceitful, you have the high ground; move forward.

**If you do have transforming lines:** consult those lines within this hexagram for a more direct answer. Then transform your hexagram and focus just on the **Read me first** section of the new hexagram to discover what you should do.

## Bottom line

If you have this as a transforming line, it is time to display your talents. Let people see what you can do. Open up to the situation and push on. Alternatively, if you show off it will push away the people around you (Huang). Furthermore, if you move at the wrong time you could ruin yourself (Adcock). In this situation, be strong and move forward but be careful not to aggravate people.

## Second line up

If you have this as a transforming line, now is the time to stand firm and maintain your position. Show great restraint (Huang) and take strong but steady steps forward (Adcock). However, only move if you are being righteous (Gill). In this situation, you should push forward but only if you have the correct attitude.

## Third line up

If you have this as a transforming line, use your strength to push on as long as you are sure that you are correct in what you think. If you have deceived yourself you will become trapped like a ram in a fence, thrashing about in the wrong place. A master does not run around willy-nilly but is in the correct place at the correct time (Huang), so do not waste your effort on futile endeavours. In this situation, be strong and forceful in pursuit of a goal no one can deny is for the best.

## Fourth line up

If you have this as a transforming line, find an opening and go for whatever you have in mind, having first checked to see if anything is in your way. If you are true in what you do and there is honesty in your heart, move forward and push the opposition to one side. In this situation, it is time to be forceful.

### Fifth line up

If you have this as a transforming line, it means that you have a certain degree of power and you are on the right path. Therefore, do not worry if some small things do not go your way or if you have to wait where you are for a short time. See the big picture and know that sometimes you have to be harsh, but never take things too far (Adcock). In this situation, use what power you have to achieve what you need and do not be worried by setbacks.

### Top line

If you have this as a transforming line, it means the situation you are in right now is not going to allow you to move forwards or backwards. You have to stand firm and stay where you are. Make no moves and wait for things to change before you move on. In this situation, immediately stop so that you do not make a mistake; wait for a while before casting again.

## HEXAGRAM 35

**This hexagram represents: promoting and advancing**

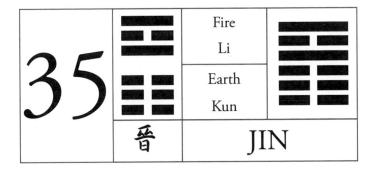

### READ ME FIRST

This hexagram appearing in your casting means that you have some prospects for progress in the situation you are asking about. The lower trigram is **Earth** and the upper trigram is **Fire**. The image is of the light rising at dawn; like sunrise you are in a phase of upward movement.

**If you do not have any transforming lines:** this hexagram does not necessarily mean that you will advance, but there is an opening for you if you do the right thing. Therefore, if you keep moving forward and act with integrity you should be successful in what you aim to do. This time is all about pushing on, but doing so in the correct way.

**If you do have transforming lines:** consult those lines within this hexagram for a more direct answer. Then transform your hexagram and focus just on the **Read me first** section of the new hexagram to discover what you should do.

### Bottom line

If you have this as a transforming line, look out for any jealous reactions to something positive happening within the situation you are in. Your happiness or success may annoy others. Therefore, remain calm and steadfast in your forward movement (Huang) but be on guard for hot tempers or cold malignancy. In this situation, be careful about igniting envy in others; you can still get to where you want to be, but do so without causing aggravation.

### Second line up

If you have this as a transforming line, you should take a step forward within your situation if you have the opportunity to do so. There is no need to worry about what others may think. No matter what the question asked, do not hold back for the sake of anyone else; this is your chance to get ahead. Move forward with purity and it will be well (Huang) and seek help from someone close, who will most likely be female. However, do not compromise your ideals if something feels off to you (Adcock). In this situation, you should push on with help from an ally.

### Third line up

If you have this as a transforming line, a positive development in the future will help to dispel negativity from the past. If all people can move together as one nothing bad will come of it (Gill). Do not worry if you need help, but always give credit where credit is due (Adcock). In this situation, jump onto anything positive and acknowledge other people's contribution to your success.

### Fourth line up
If you have this as a transforming line, show other people that you have the skills and attitude to manage the situation by yourself. People may think you do not deserve to succeed, but you can show them that you do. However, if you act without clear goals it will cause problems (Huang). Therefore, do not dilly-dally, but be direct and forthright (Gill). Do not act selfishly (Adcock). In this situation, show people that you are equipped to achieve your aims.

### Fifth line up
If you have this as a transforming line, you are in a good position to do what you need to do. Do not "sweat the small stuff"; just carry on with your plans and any minor issues will resolve themselves. You might not realize it, but you have come a long way already (Adcock). In this situation, recognize what you have achieved so far, push any problems to the side and keep going.

### Top line
If you have this as a transforming line, stand your ground and stop those around you from causing trouble. Do not be rude or overbearing, but be strong and fair. Have the self-control not to move forward if there is danger (Huang); do not be aggressive (Gill); and do not abuse your power (Adcock). In this situation, it is time for you to assert yourself and stop people from overstepping their mark.

## HEXAGRAM 36

**This hexagram represents: hiding your talent and dark times**

| 36 | | Earth Kun | |
| --- | --- | --- | --- |
| | | Fire Li | |
| | 明夷 | MING YI | |

READ ME FIRST

This hexagram appearing in your casting means that the powers of darkness, meanness and cruelty are on the rise. The lower trigram is **Fire** and the upper trigram is **Earth**. The image here is that the light has gone over the horizon and night has set in.

**If you do not have any transforming lines:** this is not a time to shine. Blend in with the crowd and hide your intentions and abilities so that you do not make yourself a target for those who may wish you harm. Retreat into your cave and sit it out for a while. Ignore any temptation to emerge; defence and hiding are your best options here.

**If you do have transforming lines:** consult those lines within this hexagram for a more direct answer. Then transform your hexagram and focus just on the **Read me first** section of the new hexagram to discover what you should do.

### Bottom line

If you have this as a transforming line, lie low for a while and try not to be too discouraged if someone or something has brought you down and put you in a dark place. Things will change with time, so be patient. In this situation, if things have gone sour just keep quiet and wait for the sweetness to return.

### Second line up

If you have this as a transforming line, there may be dark forces set against you. Find allies to support you in your fight. Also, help others in their times of darkness if you can (Crisp), but never compromise your principles no matter what (Adcock). In this situation, find people to help you through any negative issues.

### Third line up

If you have this as a transforming line, it is time to battle the dark forces that are rising against you. Now is not a time to be passive. However, do not fight in enemy territory (Gill) and understand that it is acceptable to get help (Adcock). In this situation, do not let anyone bully you or be overbearing; stand up for yourself.

### Fourth line up

If you have this as a transforming line, you are in a bad situation and you should get out of there before things take a turn for the worse. Avoid any "storms" in society or within your social circle (Crisp). You are in a bad position to make a move, so put your plans on hold (Gill). Also, avoid selfish deeds at this time (Adcock). In this situation, step away from the action; you are not in a good position to do what you want to.

### Fifth line up

If you have this as a transforming line, it is time to hide what you think and be careful of what you say. Do not let anyone know your plans. Although you are in a tough position and you are not able to advance, stand true and do not abandon anyone or anything. Alternatively, even if you see injustice or you know something is wrong, now is not the time to fight it (Crisp). In this situation, go fully on the defensive; help defend others but do not expose yourself to danger and make sure people cannot read your intentions.

### Top line

If you have this as a transforming line, be very wary of offers that seem too good to be true. Whatever situation you are in, there is twisted malevolence around you. It would be all too easy to step into a trap. But remember the sun will come out again, so keep up your hopes for another time (Crisp). And, of course, never abuse your power (Adcock). In this situation, it would be best to resist temptation.

## HEXAGRAM 37

**This hexagram represents: family, clan and the household**

| 37 | | Wind Xun | |
| | | Fire Li | |
| 家人 | | JIA REN | |

**READ ME FIRST**

This hexagram appearing in your casting means that you should know your correct place within any situation. The lower trigram is **Fire** and the upper trigram is **Wind**. The image is of a warm atmosphere radiating throughout a house from the fire at its centre.

**If you do not have any transforming lines:** whatever you are doing, whether on your own or in a group, you need cohesion, clarity and direction. Truthfully consider where your rightful place is so that you do not step on other people's toes. Ask yourself what is not working within your ideas, and fix those parts that are out of sync.

**If you do have transforming lines:** consult those lines within this hexagram for a more direct answer. Then transform your hexagram and focus just on the **Read me first** section of the new hexagram to discover what you should do.

### Bottom line

If you have this as a transforming line, you should clarify the situation and its parameters. It may be that a lack of understanding of the situation, either in your own mind or collectively within a group of people, is causing a problem. Take time to clear things up. From the very start of a venture or idea, hold firm to clarity and structure (Huang). In this situation, explaining things clearly to yourself and others will solve problems.

### Second line up

If you have this as a transforming line, work out how to divide responsibilities within the group. Too many people trying to do the same thing is confusing and inefficient. Share out tasks fairly and appropriately. If there is no group and you are working on your own, make sure you are not trying to do too many things at once and that you focus on the task in hand. If you nurture each and every member of a group it will benefit you (Crisp). Make sure you are not aggressive or the people around you will feel the negativity (Adcock). Keep people focused on the essential matters; there is a danger that they will become distracted by things that are not connected to the situation (Gill). In this situation, simplification and organization are the watchwords.

### Third line up

If you have this as a transforming line, now is a time to tighten up your approach to the situation in question, whether this relates just to yourself or a wider group. Things appear to have become too slack. It is not good to always be too rigid, but this moment calls for proper hard work. To maintain harmony for all, be neither too firm nor too lax (Huang). Be firm in what you do and say but also make sure that you are fair (Adcock). Clear the air with people rather than letting disagreements fester (Gill). In this situation, pick up the slack but do not tighten things to breaking point.

### Fourth line up

If you have this as a transforming line, good fortune will come if you work well with the others in your group. If you are doing something alone make sure that you are cohesive in your own mind. One unhappy member of the group will cause problems for all. Also, dig deep and ask yourself what your real motives are for what you are doing (Adcock). In this situation, keep everyone in the group happy as any negativity risks destroying the good that you are doing.

### Fifth line up

If you have this as a transforming line, make sure that your personal, group or family administration is correct and well ordered. Establish clear, sensible rules and guidelines within your home, work and relationships. Harmony within any situation brings about positivity (Huang). In this situation, double check that all the working parts of your plan are running smoothly.

## Top line

If you have this as a transforming line, politely but firmly let other people know what is expected of them, or understand what is expected of yourself. Good leadership is the basis for good outcomes, and vice versa. If you are the leader, make sure you are approachable. In this situation, practise, or advocate for, good leadership with fair rules and clear objectives.

# HEXAGRAM 38

**This hexagram represents: misunderstanding, disagreement and division**

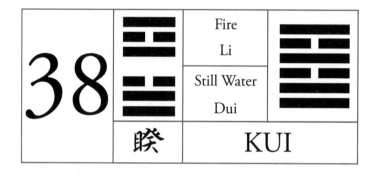

| 38 | | Fire<br>Li | |
| | | Still Water<br>Dui | |
| | 睽 | KUI | |

READ ME FIRST

This hexagram appearing in your casting indicates that you may be in a phase of disagreement. Whether someone is misunderstanding you or you are misunderstanding them, something is not connecting correctly. The lower trigram is **Still Water** and the upper trigram is **Fire**. Pearson sees this incongruous image of fire above water as representing nature gone awry; things have moved out of their normal alignment. Huang observes that fire naturally moves upward, while water moves downward, so this hexagram represents two aspects diverging, just as humans who argue move away from each other. Conversely, Crisp sees this hexagram as apparent opposites coming together.

**If you do not have any transforming lines:** correct any misunderstandings in other people or try to see the situation from their point of view. It may be that it is you who is seeing the situation incorrectly. Question your assumptions and take a fresh look. Work hard to overcome any disagreements at this time.

**If you do have transforming lines:** consult those lines within this hexagram for a more direct answer. Then transform your hexagram and focus just on the **Read me first** section of the new hexagram to discover what you should do.

### Bottom line
If you have this as a transforming line, step back from any disagreements and take the heat out of the situation. Do not react to people who are against you at the moment; they will do you little harm. At this time, do not chase anything; relax and take a step back (Crisp). In this situation, ease up and let things settle down.

### Second line up
If you have this as a transforming line, address any disagreements before they escalate. You do not want them to lead to a split. Maintain good relations even within an argument. Keep your heart open to compromise and differing viewpoints (Huang). In this situation, heal divisions or it will not go well.

### Third line up
If you have this as a transforming line, do not worry about aggressive people and naysayers who may try to dismantle your plans. Let them burn themselves out; you will come out on top in the end. Alternatively, being too weak or too aggressive is a problem for you here (Adcock). In this situation, outlast those who want to stop you; if you persevere you will win.

### Fourth line up
If you have this as a transforming line, there is someone who will support you if you need it but they may not be in the most obvious place. If times are getting hard, look for the person who will help you bring light to it. Have faith and be open to meeting the people you need to meet (Adcock). In this situation, you need to have people on your side.

### Fifth line up

If you have this as a transforming line, there is a long-standing issue from the past that is holding you back. You will not move forward until you let go of that grudge. If one of your friends stands by you firmly, treat that person with a deep respect. If someone is trying to make amends with you, look on them with a kind heart. Stick to the truth but do not be dogmatic (Adcock). In this situation, holding on to an old problem will make new ones.

### Top line

If you have this as a transforming line, someone who may appear to be against you is actually an ally. A person who gives you an alternative opinion is not your enemy. Maybe you should listen to them. It is time to make a friend of a person who talks honestly (Huang). Also, if you are at odds with a friend, remember why you became friends with them to begin with (Crisp). Your feelings of paranoia are unfounded (Adcock). In this situation, friends who see things differently from you are an asset.

## HEXAGRAM 39

**This hexagram represents: obstruction, impediment and overcoming**

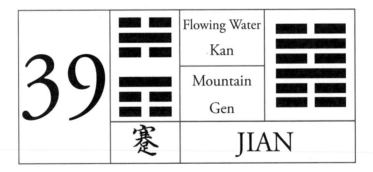

| 39 | Flowing Water Kan | |
|---|---|---|
| | Mountain Gen | |
| 蹇 | JIAN | |

**READ ME FIRST**

This hexagram appearing in your casting represents adversity or something opposing you. The lower trigram is **Mountain** and the upper trigram is **Flowing Water**. The image is of a mountain obstructing the flow of water. Huang says that a rushing river to cross and a craggy mountain to climb both represent difficult challenges to overcome.

**If you do not have any transforming lines:** you may need help to find the answer; your own resources may not be enough. There is an obstacle in the way, and you have to decide whether it is worth your trouble to get over it or not, whether you need to get help or not, or whether you have to help others. Therefore stop, think and replan before you move on.

**If you do have transforming lines:** consult those lines within this hexagram for a more direct answer. Then transform your hexagram and focus just on the **Read me first** section of the new hexagram to discover what you should do.

### Bottom line
If you have this as a transforming line, now is time to wait or move slowly. Do not act in haste. If you need to ask something of someone, do it gently and with subtlety. Also, find an easier way to achieve your goal than the solution you have in mind (Crisp). In this situation, consider taking a more indirect route to get you where you want.

### Second line up
If you have this as a transforming line, stand by your word. If you have said that you will do something, do it. If you have promises outstanding, fulfil them, even if this damages your situation somewhat. Even if you do not see it as your responsibility to deal with this situation, it is best that you just get on with it (Crisp). Do not blame others for problems that are your fault (Adcock). In this situation, do what needs to be done without quibbling.

### Third line up
If you have this as a transforming line, this is not a great time to move into action. Wait for a better opportunity. It may be that this challenge is too much for you, and there is no shame in admitting it (Crisp). In this situation, ask yourself in all seriousness whether you can actually achieve what you want to do.

### Fourth line up
If you have this as a transforming line, it means that what you are facing is too difficult to accomplish alone. You must find help. Be patient and the

situation will turn to your advantage over time. In this situation, do not attempt the task by yourself.

### Fifth line up

If you have this as a transforming line, seek help from trusted friends rather than looking for new people to assist you. In this situation, rely on the people who are already at hand; do not try to find help from the outside.

### Top line

If you have this as a transforming line, listen to the advice of someone who knows more about the issue in question before going into action. Make no move until you know what you are doing. If it turns out that you are the expert that someone else is seeking to help with their problem, be generous with your time and knowledge. In this situation, either be the expert and give your time, or ask an expert to give you their time.

## HEXAGRAM 40

**This hexagram represents: separation, release, liberation and relief**

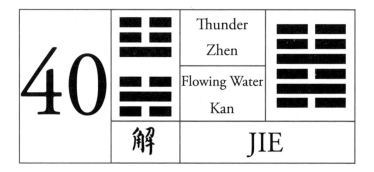

| | | Thunder Zhen | |
| --- | --- | --- | --- |
| 40 | | Flowing Water Kan | |
| | 解 | JIE | |

This hexagram appearing in your casting means that you should not let others hold you back. Separate from them if you need to and advance on your own within this situation. The lower trigram is **Flowing Water** and the upper trigram is **Thunder**. The image is of thunder and rain, but also carries the promise of clear skies after the storm has passed. Huang sees the point of this hexagram being that you have to separate the negative from the positive in any situation, while Gill sees it as representing an action that you must take right away to move on to the next stage. Crisp says that like a cloud releases its rain, you must let go of what is weighing you down so you can move on.

**If you do not have any transforming lines:** identify what is holding you back and detach yourself from it. Sometimes it is better to go it alone. You may have to leave friends behind but perhaps only until they can catch up with you.

**If you do have transforming lines:** consult those lines within this hexagram for a more direct answer. Then transform your hexagram and focus just on the **Read me first** section of the new hexagram to discover what you should do.

### Bottom line
If you have this as a transforming line, go on ahead even though separating from others is hard. If you have just got through a difficult experience take steps to prevent it happening again (Adcock). In this situation, have the courage to go it alone.

### Second line up
If you have this as a transforming line, move ahead but with small steps. Going all out may damage your relations with other people. Ignore false praise, as it is bad for you (Adcock). In this situation, go your own way with caution.

### Third line up
If you have this as a transforming line, it is a warning not to channel all of your efforts into a single area. Keep several different avenues open. Make sure that your actions match your words (Huang) and do not let your pride and ego trip you up (Adcock). Showing off will annoy other people (Gill). In this situation, try different approaches rather than becoming fixated on one path.

### Fourth line up
If you have this as a transforming line, push forward right away. If you hold on to the past you will not move forward (Adcock). Therefore, let go of

anyone or anything dragging you back (Crisp). In this situation, cast off all hindrances from your past and move directly into action without waiting.

## Fifth line up

If you have this as a transforming line, go forward and make your ideas public to gain support from others. Stay away from people who want to bring you down or lead you along the wrong path (Huang). Release yourself from bad habits and old ideas (Adcock). In this situation, press ahead and the people who need to will catch up with you.

## Top line

If you have this as a transforming line, identify who or what is holding you back or blocking the way. Once you have removed that barrier you will see a clear road ahead of you. Be aware that the obstacle may lie within yourself, in the form of your own ego or a negative thought you are struggling to let go of (Adcock). You have prepared all that you can, now you must move into action and do what you aim to do (Crisp). In this situation, clear all obstacles from your path and get going.

# HEXAGRAM 41

**This hexagram represents: reduction and removal**

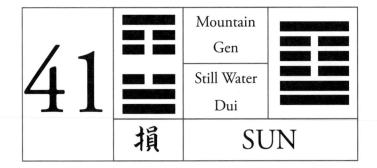

| 41 | Mountain Gen | |
| | Still Water Dui | |
| | 損 | SUN |

READ ME FIRST

This hexagram appearing in your casting implies diminishing, lessening or decreasing. It means that you may have to remove something from the situation. The lower trigram is **Still Water** and the upper trigram is **Mountain**. The image here is of still water in a lake evaporating to reveal more and more of the base of the mountain. Gill says that as the rain water flows off the mountain it is removed from the slopes but fills the lake below. Adcock says that things cannot forever be increasing, nor should you want them to; sometimes you have to let go of your gains and start afresh.

**If you do not have any transforming lines:** there is something within your present circumstances which needs to decrease. This may not go down well with others who are used to having what they have, so if you need to take something away from someone explain why you need to take it away. If you do it honestly and with integrity people will understand.

**If you do have transforming lines:** consult those lines within this hexagram for a more direct answer. Then transform your hexagram and focus just on the **Read me first** section of the new hexagram to discover what you should do.

## Bottom line

If you have this as a transforming line, put your time and effort into your friends or others who are close to you. Help those around you (Adcock) and take time out from your own activities to see what others are doing (Crisp). Keep good judgement on how much you should get rid of and how much you should keep, be it friends, possessions, ideas and so on (Gill). In this situation, decrease your self-focus and increase your attention on others.

## Second line up

If you have this as a transforming line, be careful how much you "spend" – whether this be time, money, effort and so on. Reduce your output; whatever you are doing may burn you out or use up all of your resources. Put equal amounts of effort into yourself and others (Huang), but do not help others if you consider what they are doing to be a lost cause or a waste of time (Crisp). Be fair in all you decide (Gill). Also, be careful not to help others so much that it affects your goals (Adcock). In this situation, check your resources and make sure you have more coming in than going out, no matter what it is.

### Third line up

If you have this as a transforming line, you need to reduce the number of people or elements within the situation. It could be that your mind or life is overcrowded with different people, plans and projects. Free up space, time and resources by decreasing what you think is hindering you. In this situation, get rid of something to allow space for something better.

### Fourth line up

If you have this as a transforming line, look for ways to improve the situation. This whole hexagram is about decreasing something to allow for things to prosper. Celebrate the things you have done that have had a positive effect. Look to a true friend to help you take on some of your burdens (Huang). Understand that it is time to break any bad habits (Crisp). You may have to ask for help (Gill). In this situation, see what is actually helping you and focus on that, while moving on from things that do not help.

### Fifth line up

If you have this as a transforming line, make sure that you recognize the good efforts of people who look up to you as a leader or guide. Stay modest and true, otherwise you will not progress (Huang). In this situation, if you ignore those who are helping you they will leave you in a muddle.

### Top line

If you have this as a transforming line, it means that this is actually a time to increase not decrease. Go that extra mile. Raise your spending, boost your effort, give the situation all the attention you have. Also, consider whether you would prefer to do this alone or with others (Crisp). Try to find a way to gain what you need without taking from others (Gill). In this situation, it is time to add what is needed to push the situation forward, but it must come from you not others.

# HEXAGRAM 42

**This hexagram represents: increasing and expansion**

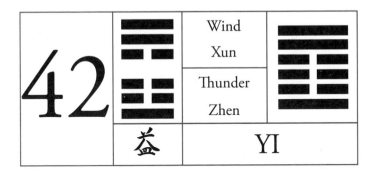

| 42 | Wind Xun / Thunder Zhen | |
|---|---|---|
| | 益 | YI |

**READ ME FIRST**

This hexagram appearing in your casting means that you are in a period of prosperity and you should look to spend your "wealth". This does not have to be money; it could be energy, time – anything that is either increasing or in abundance and can be used to help you get to where you want to go. The lower trigram is **Thunder** and the upper trigram is **Wind**. The image here is of wind and thunder combining to produce a force far greater than each of them on their own.

**If you do not have any transforming lines:** like the two powerful forces of thunder and wind, at this time you are increasing in power, so use what you have to push you forward to the next stage in achieving your goal. Gill uses the alternative "wood" translation of the **Wind** trigram, seeing the hexagram as representing thunder (or lightning) surging up through a tree and filling it with power. Similarly, you are at this point filled with increasing energy and ability. If you wish to go in a certain direction, no matter what, plunge in and enjoy yourself. It may be time to let your resources of money, love, power or whatever flow out from you to make for better returns in the future. Or it may be that you still have to build up more. Focus on what you have and what you should do with it.

**If you do have transforming lines:** consult those lines within this hexagram for a more direct answer. Then transform your hexagram and focus just on the **Read me first** section of the new hexagram to discover what you should do.

### Bottom line

If you have this as a transforming line, you should loosen your grip on your resources and let them flow out. This could be time, energy, money and so on. There is something you have enough of, so give it out and then you can take the next step. In this situation, hoarding will get you nowhere.

### Second line up

If you have this as a transforming line, give back something in return for what has been given to you. What goes out comes back, maybe in a different form, but it will start the ball rolling. If you receive something at this time be truly thankful and treat it as a gift from heaven (Huang). Make sure to look out for fate giving you a push in the right direction (Adcock). In this situation, give out to the world and the world will give back to you.

### Third line up

If you have this as a transforming line, take support from others to do what you need to do. This could be money, time, effort, energy and so on. In short, you need help to achieve your aims. If a beneficial or troublesome situation arises out of the blue, know that it has been put there by the universe either to spur you on or to test you (Crisp). If you have made a mistake here, treat it as a good lesson (Adcock). In this situation, do not be too proud or shy to get help.

### Fourth line up

If you have this as a transforming line, you may have to take a different approach to the problem or challenge you are facing. Make sure that you give fairly to all people and do not push yourself to an extreme position (Crisp). If someone wants to give you more responsibility, be confident that you have the ability to take it on (Gill). If other people ask you for help do not deny them, but also be honest about how much you are able to help them (Adcock). In this situation, look for another way to get to where you want to go and do not be daunted if it is a difficult path.

## Fifth line up

If you have this as a transforming line, know that all you have to do is be good in your life, do the right thing and opportunities will open up for you. In this situation, return to the centre and clean the slate.

## Top line

If you have this as a transforming line, be careful as there are people out there who disagree with what you want to do and may want to stop you doing it. Also, be conscious that it may be you who is trying to block someone else on their path. If you are not true in your heart, others will not warm to you (Huang). If you hoard what you have it will jam up your path and heaven will turn away, so be generous (Crisp). Make sure what you want to achieve is righteous, otherwise the universe will put a stop to it (Gill). In this situation, ask yourself whether someone else is trying to stop you or whether you are trying to stop them.

# HEXAGRAM 43

**This hexagram represents: severing ties, being resolute and moving on**

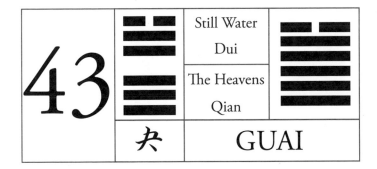

| 43 | Still Water Dui | |
| --- | --- | --- |
| | The Heavens Qian | |
| 夬 | GUAI | |

**READ ME FIRST**

This hexagram appearing in your casting suggests a breaking of ties or bonds or the ending of a relationship. The lower trigram is **The Heavens** and the upper trigram is **Still Water**. The modern commentators do not all agree on the meaning of this image. The Chinese character, which is extremely rare and no longer used in modern Chinese, means "eliminating" or "severing" or "eliminating any hesitation you have". Huang says that this is concerned with the evaporation of water and the releasing of pressure from society, for when water evaporates into the sky it severs its connection with the ground.

**If you do not have any transforming lines:** tread with caution and start to talk in a non-confrontational way to other people involved to ease the situation. This time is about deciding what to let go of and how to do it in a positive way. Find new ways, but do not abandon the old ways that are still working.

**If you do have transforming lines:** consult those lines within this hexagram for a more direct answer. Then transform your hexagram and focus just on the **Read me first** section of the new hexagram to discover what you should do.

### Bottom line

If you have this as a transforming line, it means you need support from a more powerful person or you need to get yourself into a more powerful position before you make a move. If you move into action now you could fail, so think carefully about whether you want to risk it (Crisp). Understand what your real abilities are and do not lie to yourself about them (Adcock). In this situation, build a stronger power base before you act.

### Second line up

If you have this as a transforming line, now is the time to fully concentrate on the situation. If you are not vigilant things will not go well for you. Stay alert and keep an eye out for any changes that are being made. Understand that you may not have the strength to do everything that you want right now, so find a middle way that gets you a little further on (Huang). Take extra care to look out for dangers which are coming your way (Adcock and Crisp). In this situation, focus on all the details of what is happening around you to avoid falling into difficulty.

### Third line up

If you have this as a transforming line, you may be in a bad situation. Perhaps you have broken ties with someone or acquired a new enemy. If so, just ride it out. Now is the time to be strong. Current problems will soon fall into the past, so you do not have to heed them. Be careful not to attach yourself to the wrong people or situation, as it might leave you with a bad reputation (Crisp). Do not be pressured into doing something you are not sure about (Adcock). In this situation, stay strong and do what you believe to be right, not what other people want you to do.

## Fourth line up

If you have this as a transforming line, understand that if you have suffered a downfall or something is not going your way the fault is yours. Just accept it. It is time to learn from your mistakes and make sure that you do not go down that path again. Perhaps find someone to help you break away from any bad aspects of your life (Huang). But do not rush, as you may make even bigger mistakes in your haste (Crisp). If you are not careful you could turn people against you (Adcock). In this situation, accept your share of the blame for what has gone wrong and seek support from others to move on.

## Fifth line up

If you have this as a transforming line, weed out the problems in your life. You are bogged down with attachments or people that are holding you back. Therefore, get rid of anything that is not positive in your life but do it in a gentle way without malice so you do not create future enemies. If you see people making mistakes do not be too harsh on them; help them improve (Adcock). In this situation, eliminate the aspects of your life that are dragging you down.

## Top line

If you have this as a transforming line, you will have to wait for your ideas or goals to come to fruition. Maybe it is time to move on from outdated ideas and look for a new goal or a new path to the existing goal. However, do not relax your attention or you may lose any gains you have achieved (Crisp). It seems at this time that there is no one who will help you (Gill). Therefore, remain disciplined at this time and do not lose focus (Adcock). In this situation, look for a better way to do what you want but without losing the ground you have covered so far.

# HEXAGRAM 44

**This hexagram represents: meeting and coming together**

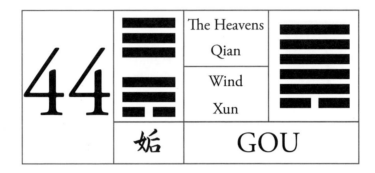

This hexagram appearing in your casting relates to interacting and engaging socially with people. The lower trigram is **Wind** and the upper trigram is **The Heavens**. The image here is of the wind beneath the sky blowing everywhere and coming into contact with everyone and everything. The original Chinese character refers to a royal bride, a woman or the feminine aspect in general. Various commentators have speculated as to whether this is seen in a positive light or a negative one – this aspect has been removed here.

**If you do not have any transforming lines:** look for inspiring people who can lead you to where you want to be, but make sure that they are genuine. Remember that the people you mix with will shape your attitude and that could turn out to be a problem. You need to look deeply into the intentions of those around you to know how to interact with them.

**If you do have transforming lines:** consult those lines within this hexagram for a more direct answer. Then transform your hexagram and focus just on the **Read me first** section of the new hexagram to discover what you should do.

### Bottom line

If you have this as a transforming line, you should be really careful about who you get involved with. The correct people will help you answer the question you have; the wrong people will destroy your dreams. Anyone can do damage to you and your cause, so look out (Crisp). It might be time to restrain yourself from going too far (Gill). Stop any problems before they get bigger (Adcock). In this situation, seek the right people; any movement in the wrong direction, either by yourself or by others, could seriously damage your position.

### Second line up

If you have this as a transforming line, check the intentions of those around you. Negative or harmful people will jeopardize what you are trying to achieve. Make sure you have ways to control the situation so that things do not go bad. In this situation, observe what everyone is doing and detect any hidden attacks.

### Third line up

If you have this as a transforming line, there may be someone around you who has a bad secret in their past. Maybe they have changed their ways but just be careful about people and their true intentions. If you have had a bad experience, make sure you do everything to avoid the same thing happening again (Gill). If the pressure is too much find a still place to calm down (Adcock). In this situation, consider people's pasts and judge whether they pose a problem for you now.

### Fourth line up

If you have this as a transforming line, someone who has just entered the situation you are in may be no good for you or those around you. Look to everyone and see what their intentions are, especially anyone new. If you support others, they will support you (Huang). Do not just get rid of people out of hand; they may be there to help you, so investigate fully before doing anything you might regret (Crisp). Avoid becoming intolerant (Adcock). In this situation, scrutinize people who have recently arrived in your life or your situation.

Page 210

## Fifth line up

If you have this as a transforming line, your path has been unblocked and so now may be the time to press forward. However, be careful that you do not come across as too forceful or confident. Stay grounded and live virtuously (Huang). Have confidence in others if you want them to have confidence in you (Crisp). In this situation, move forward purposefully but without drawing undue attention to yourself.

## Top line

If you have this as a transforming line, discourage others from pushing your profile forward or advancing your cause too vigorously. Welcome help from others but use it correctly, taking care not to be too aggressive (Gill). Fight the battles you have to fight, but avoid unnecessary conflicts (Adcock). In this situation, stay in control but with a light touch.

# HEXAGRAM 45

**This hexagram represents: gathering and mingling**

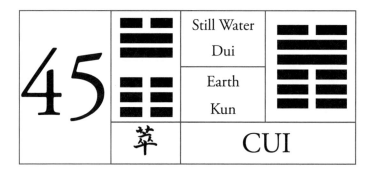

This hexagram appearing in your casting represents people assembling, a uniting of the many. The lower trigram is **Earth** and the upper trigram is **Still Water**. The image is of water rising and collecting together, as separate ponds, streams and rivers together form into a powerful water system.

**If you do not have any transforming lines:** now is the time to bring people together. Pick the people you need to help you survive or thrive.

Be careful not to rub people the wrong way. It is important that you see things from their point of view. Sometimes you may have to push ahead of people, at other times you may have to wait for them to catch up, but overall you should focus on bringing people together.

**If you do have transforming lines:** consult those lines within this hexagram for a more direct answer. Then transform your hexagram and focus just on the **Read me first** section of the new hexagram to discover what you should do.

### Bottom line
If you have this as a transforming line, the goal you want to achieve is correct. Gather your supporters and go forward with sincere intent. If you are hesitating to engage with a certain person or people, overcome your suspicions; the union will be positive (Crisp). However, make sure your ideas benefit everyone (Adcock). Do not be afraid to ask to join a group you want to get involved with (Gill). In this situation, do not let doubts put you off other people; all will be fine.

### Second line up
If you have this as a transforming line, do not doubt that what you are doing is correct. Move forward in the way you think is best because it is the correct thing to do. Make sure you have something to offer in the situation you are in (Crisp). Connect with people who are a natural fit (Adcock). Appreciate the benefits of forming or joining a group (Gill). In this situation, demonstrate how you can help and others will welcome you into their group.

### Third line up
If you have this as a transforming line, the people around you may not agree with your point of view. If you are having trouble relating to others, try to see the situation through their eyes and change your approach to fit better with theirs. If you feel alone, look about you and you will see a friend waiting to connect (Crisp). Let go of any grudges you may be holding (Adcock). In this situation, look at the situation from other angles and adjust your approach accordingly.

### Fourth line up

If you have this as a transforming line, you are absolutely on the correct path. Maintain the direction you are going in and let no one change your mind. In this situation, do what you think is correct because you are right.

### Fifth line up

If you have this as a transforming line, it may be that not everyone agrees with you, but give them time, keep an honest heart and stay true, and eventually they will come around. If the people around you are not sure about you or your intentions, be transparent and move slowly so that you do not leave them behind (Gill). However, even if no one joins you, you should still push on alone (Adcock). In this situation, give people time to get used to your ideas.

### Top line

If you have this as a transforming line, it means that while some people may not agree with your plans it is best for you to go forward anyway. Be completely honest; if you tell even white lies or half-truths at this point it will cause problems later on (Crisp). Do not allow negativity to divert you from your path (Gill). In this situation, do not let any naysayers hold you back.

## HEXAGRAM 46

**This hexagram represents: pushing upward and growing**

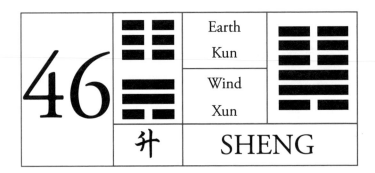

| 46 | | Earth |
| | | Kun |
| | | Wind |
| | | Xun |
| 升 | | SHENG |

READ ME FIRST

This hexagram appearing in your casting means that you are more than capable of achieving what you intend to do. You should have no problem elevating yourself to the next position. The lower trigram is **Wind** (or, in this case, **Wood**) and the upper trigram is **Earth**. The image is of vegetation breaking through the earth and rising up.

**If you do not have any transforming lines:** this is about growing as a person or moving on in a situation. It is time to progress to the next step, but be careful not to get ahead of yourself. Huang says that this is a time when you can move forward without being hindered by external obstacles; only you can cause yourself a problem.

**If you do have transforming lines:** consult those lines within this hexagram for a more direct answer. Then transform your hexagram and focus just on the **Read me first** section of the new hexagram to discover what you should do.

## Bottom line

If you have this as a transforming line, someone who has the power to help you is viewing you favourably. Do not waste the opportunity. Discover who the person is and move forward with your ambitions. In this situation, connect with people until you find the right one.

## Second line up

If you have this as a transforming line, you should do something to honour an achievement. This might mean celebrating how far you have come or how well someone else is doing. Either way, now is the time to give back to the community by providing a "feast" of any type. Even a modest celebration is worth doing (Crisp). In this situation, gather people together to acknowledge what has been achieved so far, in order to propel you to the next step.

## Third line up

If you have this as a transforming line, whatever is facing you now will only be overcome by focusing on the fundamentals. It will be hard work and you may need to build from the ground up. There is nothing actually standing in your way (Gill), but you will only succeed by following or setting a good example (Adcock). In this situation, start from the beginning, use basic building blocks and strong foundations to complete the whole journey.

### Fourth line up

If you have this as a transforming line, you must put in a lot of ground work to move to the next level. Do not just "wing it" but make sure you have everything you will need. In this situation, going forward without thinking it through from all angles and preparing thoroughly will lead to failure.

### Fifth line up

If you have this as a transforming line, be careful not to get ahead of yourself. If you run too fast you will fall. Do not worry if you feel like you are going too slowly, you are making steady progress (Adcock). In this situation, slow and steady wins the day.

### Top line

If you have this as a transforming line, do not let your mind wander beyond the situation. Stay focused on what needs to be done rather than dreaming of unrealistic goals. If you push too far you may fail and lose all you have gained (Huang). Make sure the direction you are moving in is clear and correct (Crisp). The intention behind what you want to do is as important as the goal itself, so make sure your motives are correct (Adcock). In this situation, having a dream is good but what really counts is hard work and correct intentions.

## HEXAGRAM 47

**This hexagram represents: confining, oppression and exhaustion**

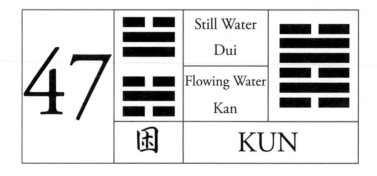

| 47 | Still Water Dui | |
| | Flowing Water Kan | |
| | 困 | KUN |

This hexagram appearing in your casting means that at the moment, while your ideas may have value, no one is willing to listen to you. It may be that you are just in the wrong place doing the wrong thing. The lower trigram is **Flowing Water** and the upper trigram is **Still Water**. The image is of slow, still water weighing itself down on moving water and stopping the flow. Movement is being blocked and energy is being sapped, leading to stagnation. Huang says that the positioning of the trigrams represents an end to the flow of moving water and a dried-up lake, meaning that you are in a period of exhaustion or you have run out of ideas to resolve the situation you are in.

**If you do not have any transforming lines:** put your ambitions on one side until this time passes. You are confined to your current position and things will not change for a while. It may be that you have got yourself into this situation. Consider different ways to get yourself out of this fix. But be patient.

**If you do have transforming lines:** consult those lines within this hexagram for a more direct answer. Then transform your hexagram and focus just on the **Read me first** section of the new hexagram to discover what you should do.

### Bottom line

If you have this as a transforming line, it means that you have got yourself into a bad position by making the wrong choices. In fact, you have come to a dead end here and it may take you a while to get out of it. Stay positive, but know that you have a long way to go (Crisp). Look within yourself for strength (Adcock). In this situation, you are stuck and pushing ahead will get you nowhere, so start moving in a different direction.

### Second line up

If you have this as a transforming line, your own faulty judgement has caused you to make a mistake. Stop what you are doing and rethink the whole situation before making your next move. Be grateful to the universe for what you have (Gill) and avoid making more mistakes. In this situation, you have got it wrong – now work out how to put it right.

### Third line up

If you have this as a transforming line, you are caught up in a situation and struggling to disentangle yourself. You need help from someone, maybe someone close, because if you do it alone it will be hard going. You have misplaced your faith, so you should not be surprised that things have gone wrong. From now on, tread carefully and keep strong. It may be that what is hampering your progress is actually your own attitude (Adcock). In this situation, find someone to help release you from this tangle.

### Fourth line up

If you have this as a transforming line, you are feeling trapped in a bad situation. It will take a long time to make any further progress along the direction you were headed so it may be better to take a different, simpler path (Crisp). You should really have seen this coming because the signs were there (Gill). Open your mind up to all possibilities (Adcock). In this situation, your escape route may be a surprising one; rule nothing out.

### Fifth line up

If you have this as a transforming line, you may have to stop what you are doing right here and change to something else. Do not fight this, you will not win. This may be a time to make some kind of sacrifice (Gill). Embrace what fate has in store for you (Adcock). In this situation, accept that you are not going to achieve your aim and that you must look elsewhere for your next challenge.

### Top line

If you have this as a transforming line, you have made a mistake and now you are stuck in a bad position. The only way out is via the moral and honest path; do not dig yourself deeper into trouble. If you accept that you have done wrong a new path will open up (Huang). It might be that you are what is holding yourself back (Adcock). In this situation, accept your share of the blame for what is not working.

# HEXAGRAM 48

**This hexagram represents: resources and replenishment**

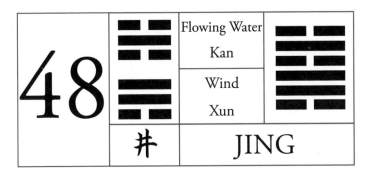

| 48 | Flowing Water Kan | | |
|---|---|---|---|
| | Wind Xun | | |
| 丼 | JING | | |

**READ ME FIRST**

This hexagram appearing in your casting means that the issue in question is related to resources that you have or do not have. This could be information, people, physical goods – anything that will help you achieve your goal. The lower trigram is **Wind** (or, in this case, **Wood**) and the upper trigram is **Flowing Water**. Pearson sees the image as a wooden frame used to draw up flowing water from a well. Huang agrees, but also sees a representation of the wood of nature drawing up water from below. In both cases, the water is being raised up high by the wood. The message is that you may need to replenish the resources that are maintaining your position. All theories rest on the idea that you need to make good use of what you have to move forward.

**If you do not have any transforming lines:** look for something or someone within your grasp to help you. The original Chinese for this hexagram means "well". Water is the resource at the centre of village life. While you can draw on it, it must be pure and clean, otherwise the whole structure of society will fail. Similarly, you need to resource your endeavours with good quality information, people and materials. If the resources are contaminated, things will turn bad.

**If you do have transforming lines:** consult those lines within this hexagram for a more direct answer. Then transform your hexagram and focus just on the **Read me first** section of the new hexagram to discover what you should do.

## Bottom line

If you have this as a transforming line, it means that you are trying to use something in the wrong way. Muddy water can be used for irrigation but not for drinking. Make sure that your resources have not been corrupted. Bad people, bad information, bad equipment and so on will lead to problems. If you do not live in accord with the aspects around you, failure will be yours (Huang). Take good care of yourself so that others can see the effort you are making (Adcock). In this situation, use the right resources in the right way.

## Second line up

If you have this as a transforming line, treat your resources with respect. If the water is good but you break your bucket you will not be able to make use of the water. Treat everyone and everything in the correct way, otherwise what you want to do will not happen. You are in the right place doing the right thing, but you need something to help you reach the next step. In this situation, make sure that everything around you is in good order so that things move forward.

## Third line up

If you have this as a transforming line, guard against neglect, waste and misuse. Take note of the talent around you and use it well (Huang); unused talent is wasted talent (Adcock). Dig deeper within your resources to find out what else you can use to make a positive difference (Gill). You may have to direct people to the things they need to help them move forward as well (Crisp). In this situation, remember that you will only be as good as the resources you have, so treat everyone and everything well or you will regret it.

## Fourth line up

If you have this as a transforming line, it is time to reorganize the way you use your resources. Something is not correct, so rethink how you are doing things. You are heading in the right direction, but like trying to get water from a broken well, you will need to change the way you get what you need (Gill). Put the effort in now and you will get where you need to be (Crisp). In this situation, restructure your operations; once you move the pieces around, everything will fall into place.

### Fifth line up

If you have this as a transforming line, you have everything working correctly so move forward with your plans. Turn your knowledge into wisdom (Adcock). In this situation, everything is in place and ready to go.

### Top line

If you have this as a transforming line, allow all your resources to work at optimum capacity. By overmanaging the situation you risk getting in the way. Like a farmer with a well brimming with clear water, you have all you need for success (Crisp). In this situation, create the conditions for your project to run smoothly, then step back and let people get on with what they do best.

## HEXAGRAM 49

**This hexagram represents: discarding the old and embracing the new**

| 49 | Still Water Dui | |
| | Fire Li | |
| 革 | GE | |

**READ ME FIRST**

This hexagram appearing in your casting means you need to reform your ideas or actions. Out with the old and in with the new. The lower trigram is **Fire** and the upper trigram is **Still Water**. The image is of fire causing water to evaporate or water dousing fire. Either way, it represents a new aspect taking over from an older one.

**If you do not have any transforming lines:** you must remember that throughout life there are times to cast off old habits. This is one of those times. There is a new way and you have to find it.

**If you do have transforming lines:** consult those lines within this hexagram for a more direct answer. Then transform your hexagram and focus just on the **Read me first** section of the new hexagram to discover what you should do.

## Bottom line

If you have this as a transforming line, remember that things of quality are made from quality materials. Inferior ideas, skills or equipment will yield inferior results. Take a look at your own performance. Is your standard high enough or do you need to improve? It is best not to act if the action is not correct (Huang). Before you make any changes, double check all elements that may not be visible at first glance (Crisp). If the goal is insurmountable, you will just waste energy trying to reach it (Gill). Building up your strength is also important (Adcock). In this situation, look to improve everything connected to your situation before you move on.

## Second line up

If you have this as a transforming line, stop procrastinating and move forward with your ideas. If you need to take action do it now, but make sure to communicate any dramatic changes clearly to others before you put them into effect (Huang). Be prepared for the results that will come about from your changes (Crisp). Take your time to make any preparations needed for change (Adcock). In this situation, change what needs to be changed, but remember sudden change can ruffle feathers.

## Third line up

If you have this as a transforming line, the people around you may not understand what you want to do. You may have to present your aims and goals in a new way. Eventually people will catch on. Explain and explain again, so no mistakes are made (Gill). Getting it done right is more important than getting it done quickly (Adcock). In this situation, be totally sure that everyone understands what you want to do before you proceed.

## Fourth line up

If you have this as a transforming line, correct any mistakes you may have made as soon as possible. Making even minor improvements to your approach can deliver great results. Try to establish a better way (Crisp) and watch all blockages fall away before you (Gill). If you want sustained success, you have to have good motives (Adcock). In this situation, fine tune the details to make the overall plan work.

### Fifth line up

If you have this as a transforming line, it means you are doing the right thing. Like a tiger on the prowl, you instinctively know when to pounce. In this situation, trust in your natural abilities and you will not fail.

### Top line

If you have this as a transforming line, try to tell the difference between people who are genuinely trying to help you and those who are only pretending and may even be out to hinder you. You need people you can rely on to get you to the next step. Be mindful that some people take a long time to accept change (Huang). Remember that if you are not dedicated to your goals, no one else will be (Crisp). Make small adjustments that will lead to significant improvements (Adcock). In this situation, identify your genuine supporters and give people time to adapt to new ways of doing things.

# HEXAGRAM 50

**This hexagram represents: establishing something new**

| 50 | Fire Li | |
| | Wind Xun | |
| 鼎 | DING | |

**READ ME FIRST**

This hexagram appearing in your casting means that you should identify which parts of your life or goals are solid and which parts need changing.

The lower trigram is **Wind** (or, in this case, **Wood**) and the upper trigram is **Fire**. The image is of a large cauldron, with wood feeding the fire below the cooking pot. In ancient China, a cauldron would stand on legs and it had two handles so that it could be lifted. In later days the Chinese character for this hexagram came to mean "establishing something new". The idea is that if one of the legs of the cauldron breaks, the food spills out, while if one of the handles snaps off, you cannot move the cauldron, so you should replace what is in bad condition before it causes a problem.

**If you do not have any transforming lines:** when everything or everyone is doing their job properly things work out well, but if something is at breaking point it would be best to replace it before it does break. Look to all the parts of your life at the moment and see what is robust and what is ready to snap. That is where you will find your answer.

**If you do have transforming lines:** consult those lines within this hexagram for a more direct answer. Then transform your hexagram and focus just on the **Read me first** section of the new hexagram to discover what you should do.

## Bottom line

If you have this as a transforming line, get rid of rotten ideas and bring yourself up to date. Contamination can spread, so it is best to cut it out before it spoils everything else. You may be reluctant to part with things that you have had for a long time, but it is time to rethink what you really need. In this situation, have a deep clean and look for a better way to do things.

## Second line up

If you have this as a transforming line, ignore any individuals who are against you, as they are inconsequential. Worrying about negative people gives them power over you, so cut off their fuel source. Do not worry about what people say; they are just jealous (Adcock). In this situation, ignore criticism and negativity and push on no matter what.

## Third line up

If you have this as a transforming line, things may be difficult for a while. Like a large food vessel that has lost one of its handles, you are full of good things but struggling to deliver them. Prepare yourself for hard work. Rewards will come in time, so there is no need to search them out (Adcock). Make it easier for other people to get involved (Crisp). In this situation, understand that your big ideas need a lot of effort to make them a reality.

## Fourth line up

If you have this as a transforming line, there is a possibility that your plans will fall apart if you do not pay attention to every last detail. Allow only people with the correct skills to deal with any part of what you are doing (Huang). Do not take on more than you can handle (Adcock). In this situation, if you overcommit yourself you may neglect something important.

## Fifth line up

If you have this as a transforming line, replace nasty old aspects of the situation with shiny new ones. The old ways are not always great; sometimes a new system is needed. In this situation, replace negatives with positives.

## Top line

If you have this as a transforming line, find a balance between doing too little and going over the top. Idleness will not serve you, but ostentation and over-elaboration are shallow; what is best in life is to look for simple things that work well (Gill). It seems that the universe is shining a light on your ideas so stay positive (Crisp). In this situation, have faith in the universe and approach things in a simple, stripped-down way.

# HEXAGRAM 51

**This hexagram represents: startling change, turbulence and reaction**

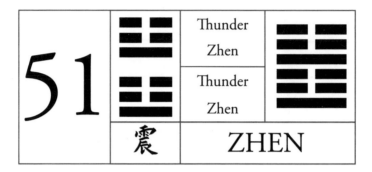

| 51 | Thunder Zhen | |
| | Thunder Zhen | |
| 震 | ZHEN | |

READ ME FIRST

This hexagram appearing in your casting means that something new and unexpected is either happening or about to happen. The lower and upper trigrams are both **Thunder**. The image is of dynamic change, instant shock, an action that compels people to change and so on.

**If you do not have any transforming lines:** consider how each situation influences yourself and the people around you. When change does occur, often people do not change with it and they become stuck in the past. Your task is to ask yourself what has changed and how you and others can adapt to it. The answer to your question is to be found in your own reaction to the situation or the reactions of others.

**If you do have transforming lines:** consult those lines within this hexagram for a more direct answer. Then transform your hexagram and focus just on the **Read me first** section of the new hexagram to discover what you should do.

**Bottom line**
If you have this as a transforming line, something that has caused a stir in your life or the life of someone close to you will have an effect and it will take people time to adjust. If something new or strange is in your life or you want to do something new, understand that it will take a while to

come to terms with it. In this situation, remember that drastic changes bring trouble to the minds of most people.

### Second line up
If you have this as a transforming line, someone close to you may have left you or be leaving you. Some change has caused them to become distant from you, at least for a while. If there is distance between you and your goal, just wait. Do not chase it; eventually it will come closer to you. Do not be afraid to let go of anything; things come and go (Adcock). Accept what has happened or is going to happen and start again (Crisp). In this situation, do not mourn lost connections or missed opportunities; be patient and all will be well in the end.

### Third line up
If you have this as a transforming line, it means you have to accept new ideas. Do not be stuck in the past. If changes are afoot, look how to use them to your advantage (Adcock). If you have had a shock or a change, use it to propel yourself into action (Gill). Change is good: it wakes you up and keeps you on your toes (Crisp). In this situation, embrace change, however much of a shock it may be, and use it to push you in a new direction.

### Fourth line up
If you have this as a transforming line, it means that those who are unable to adjust to the modern world will be trapped in the past. Are you keeping up with the times? If you cannot move forward, know that you will be stuck for a while (Adcock). In this situation, let go of old ways and keep pressing ahead.

### Fifth line up
If you have this as a transforming line, move with whatever change is confronting you. At this time change is good for you. If the situation is dire, think about what you want to take into the future with you, be it ideas or objects (Gill); and be prepared to make any repairs needed to help you get back on track (Crisp). In this situation, you just have to adapt or you will not get where you want to go.

### Top line

If you have this as a transforming line, either you or someone you know is not responding to change well and this may be causing friction. Respond correctly to any change or shock, be it good or bad (Huang). Remember that change does not only represent the end of something but also the start of something new (Adcock). Be careful how you manage change, because it can affect you in negative ways (Gill). In this situation, difficulty in accepting change – either by yourself or someone close to you – is the focal point for any problems you are having.

## HEXAGRAM 52

**This hexagram represents: stopping, caution and planning**

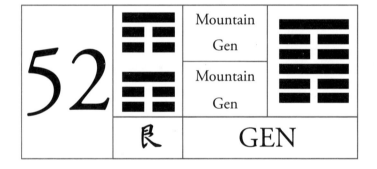

| 52 | ☶ | Mountain<br>Gen | |
| | | Mountain<br>Gen | |
| | 艮 | GEN | |

READ ME FIRST

This hexagram appearing in your casting means that you need to tackle your problem by stopping and making a plan rather than running headlong at it. The lower and upper trigrams are both **Mountain**. The image is of stillness and preparation.

**If you do not have any transforming lines:** stop, think and then decide if you should act or not when dealing with any issue currently affecting you. Acting without care at this juncture may cause more problems than you can fix. It is best to make no unplanned movements at this time.

**If you do have transforming lines:** consult those lines within this hexagram for a more direct answer. Then transform your hexagram and focus just on the **Read me first** section of the new hexagram to discover what you should do.

## Bottom line

If you have this as a transforming line, there is something you must do to help someone before they make a mistake. Or if you are about to do something then make sure you yourself are not about to go wrong. If the problem is internal, stop, think and refocus (Crisp). Resist any temptations that are presenting themselves to you (Gill). In this situation, stop anything that you have doubts about.

## Second line up

If you have this as a transforming line, be careful about getting in the way of a situation that is already in motion. Now is not the time to try to halt things as this will only cause more problems. Instead, wait for a lull in momentum before intervening. Putting up too much resistance in this situation will tire you out (Crisp). Do not blindly follow others (Adcock). In this situation, let the ball roll where it may before you try to change its direction.

## Third line up

If you have this as a transforming line, you should not act now. If you engage with the object of your goal at this time, you will cause more trouble than good. Instead, step back. If you push forward too hard you will really damage yourself (Crisp). Therefore, have restraint in all things (Gill). Avoid inflexibility; it will be no good to stand immovable before people (Adcock). In this situation, give way and do not be forceful.

## Fourth line up

If you have this as a transforming line, you must absolutely not get involved or push on with your idea. If you move forward with your intentions now you will fail miserably. Focus on healing yourself internally (Crisp). Do not let external issues affect your internal state (Adcock). In this situation, use this time to get yourself fit and ready and do not take a single step toward your goal.

### Fifth line up

If you have this as a transforming line, plan in detail how you will approach the situation you are asking about. If you make the wrong move now you will cause a lot of problems. Think before you act. Remember, you are responsible for your own actions and their consequences (Huang). It may be best to make up your own mind rather than paying too much attention to what other people think (Crisp). In this situation, stop and think before you say or do anything.

### Top line

If you have this as a transforming line, now is a time to be extremely diplomatic. Approach everyone with care and consideration. Do not be ruled by emotion. Give extra thought to what you do and say. Focus on the stillness of your mind (Gill). In this situation, treat everyone with respect and do not provoke anything.

## HEXAGRAM 53

**This hexagram represents: steady progression**

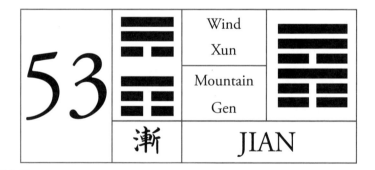

READ ME FIRST

This hexagram appearing in your casting means you should focus on sustainable progress. The lower trigram is **Mountain** and the upper trigram is **Wind** (or, in this case, **Wood**). The image is of a tree growing little by little until it is "as tall as a mountain". Pearson sees the position of the tree above the mountain in this hexagram as emphasizing its great height.

**If you do not have any transforming lines:** attend to the details, move forward slowly, consider all aspects of the situation including those that are easily overlooked. Now is a time to review the situation. Is it best to wait and rest, or "branch off" in another direction or push onward or even go beyond your original intention? Whatever you do, take your time and do not move forward with big leaps.

**If you do have transforming lines:** consult those lines within this hexagram for a more direct answer. Then transform your hexagram and focus just on the **Read me first** section of the new hexagram to discover what you should do.

### Bottom line

If you have this as a transforming line, accept any criticism that comes your way. Ask yourself how you can improve. Starting things is always difficult, but push forward and keep the faith (Crisp and Adcock). Do not pay any attention to gossip; it will not affect you (Gill). In this situation, learn from criticism and work hard to get your plan started.

### Second line up

If you have this as a transforming line, it means that you are on the right track so keep going with steady determination. Maybe take some time out to celebrate how far you have come (Crisp). In this situation, keep making steady progress along this course.

### Third line up

If you have this as a transforming line, you are going in the wrong direction. Have a rethink because if you keep doing what you are doing there will be misfortune. The harder you push in this direction, the bigger the mistake you will make (Crisp). If you do anything rash it will end in trouble (Adcock). In this situation, stop what you are doing, because it is the wrong thing.

### Fourth line up

If you have this as a transforming line, take time to regroup, look around yourself, restore your energy and think. Do not be hasty and find somewhere safe and stable (Crisp). The position you are in will not last long, so you will soon be able to move into action (Adcock). In this situation, stop for a short while to gather yourself then go again.

### Fifth line up

If you have this as a transforming line, you have done all you can in the situation you are asking about. Do not move any further forward with it. It is time to turn your gaze to new horizons. Alternatively, do not worry if the direction you are going in makes you feel isolated; just keep pushing on (Crisp). Sometimes standing apart from others gives you the freedom to do what you need to do (Adcock). In this situation, do not put any more effort into what you have been doing; it is time to try something new.

### Top line

If you have this as a transforming line, move on to the next level. Build something better by carrying on in the same direction. Alternatively, you may already have reached the finish line without realizing it and there is no need to go on (Crisp). What you are doing will inspire others (Adcock). In this situation, ask yourself whether you have done what you set out to achieve, or whether you need to keep pushing deeper.

## HEXAGRAM 54

**This hexagram represents: returning home and going back**

| 54 | Thunder Zhen | |
| | Still Water Dui | |
| 歸妹 | GUI MEI | |

READ ME FIRST

This hexagram appearing in your casting means that you have responsibilities to carry out, which may be difficult. The lower trigram is **Still Water** and the upper trigram is **Thunder**. The image is of the storm clouds carrying rain that will fill the lake back up to its normal level. Historically, this hexagram has a connection with the idea of a woman marrying and going to live in the home of her husband. It carries the notion of coming from without to within. The broader implications revolve around returning.

**If you do not have any transforming lines:** make preparations, clear your mind and look to how your actions will affect others.

**If you do have transforming lines:** consult those lines within this hexagram for a more direct answer. Then transform your hexagram and focus just on the **Read me first** section of the new hexagram to discover what you should do.

### Bottom line
If you have this as a transforming line, it means that you should assume responsibility for the situation. Even if there are other people senior to you or in a better position, now is the time to push your ideas forward. If you try to help others, they will help you (Huang). Something new in your life will make things easier for you (Crisp). In this situation, now is the time to take charge.

### Second line up
If you have this as a transforming line, think carefully about how to react to the situation. Should you step in now or wait until later or should you completely ignore it? Think through the repercussions of different responses. Be confident in your actions (Huang). If someone lets you down, do not be disheartened (Adcock). In this situation, weigh up the potential consequences of the actions you are considering.

### Third line up
If you have this as a transforming line, do not hesitate to introduce a new approach. Put your ideas into action and do not be discouraged if others are slow to adopt them. They are just nervous. Even if you feel you cannot add anything significant to a situation, do what you can because any contribution will help overall (Huang). Do not worry if you get off to a slow start; steady progress is still progress (Adcock). Maintain an open attitude and do not be enslaved by your own ideas and passions (Crisp). In

this situation, do the best you can to move forward but do not worry if it
does not get you as far as you were hoping.

### Fourth line up

If you have this as a transforming line, it means there may be a delay or
setback in your situation. Do not worry if this happens. Look at all options
before deciding how to act (Huang). Some things need time to blossom, so
be patient (Crisp). In this situation, celebrate small, slow improvements.

### Fifth line up

If you have this as a transforming line, it means a new situation has arisen
or is about to. You may not welcome this situation, but do not worry as
all will be well in the end. It might be time to avoid worldly pleasures and
cultivate your spirit instead (Huang). Sometimes other people need to take
the lead, so make sure you are not stepping on people's toes (Adcock). In
this situation, do not hate the position you are in, look to purify yourself
and be happy for others to take charge.

### Top line

If you have this as a transforming line, there may be problems you need to
navigate either now or soon. Sharpen your mind so that you are ready to
deal with the situation you are asking about. Be truthful to everyone and
there will be no confusion (Huang). Make sure you have a genuine love
for what you are asking about, otherwise it will be a waste of time (Crisp).
The situation you want may not be positive, so take care (Gill). In this
situation, preparation and a clear mind are what you need right now.

# HEXAGRAM 55

**This hexagram represents: overshadowing and abundance**

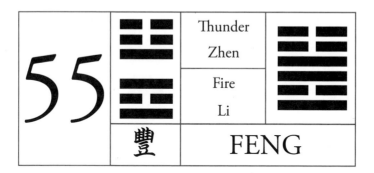

| 55 | | Thunder Zhen | |
| | | Fire Li | |
| | 豐 | FENG | |

### READ ME FIRST

This hexagram appearing in your casting means that you should enjoy the moment while it lasts. The lower trigram is **Fire** and the upper trigram is **Thunder**. The image is of fire and thunder combining to produce a powerful, fast-burning energy.

**If you do not have any transforming lines:** good and bad times come in cycles, so be aware that whatever situation you are in now will change to its opposite sooner or later. Do not become complacent during good times or despondent during bad times. Things can be ignited at this time for good or bad and there is power behind the moment. At present you are cloaked in abundance even if you do not realize it, so use it well and do not flaunt what you have in a way that will annoy other people.

**If you do have transforming lines:** consult those lines within this hexagram for a more direct answer. Then transform your hexagram and focus just on the **Read me first** section of the new hexagram to discover what you should do.

### Bottom line

If you have this as a transforming line, be wary of any changes to your relationships. When people are getting to know each other, they are often polite at first but their true feelings soon emerge. Therefore, at this time do not be overfriendly toward new people; stay on the defensive and wait to see how your interactions develop. Alternatively, share your time and energy with the people around you to build stronger bonds with them (Gill). In this situation, hold back a little when establishing ties with new people.

### Second line up

If you have this as a transforming line, do not react to people who are slandering you. Keep your distance and make sure your behaviour is beyond reproach. Your brilliance will shine through no matter what, so have faith (Adcock). In this situation, remain calm and proper even when your reputation is being questioned.

### Third line up

If you have this as a transforming line, you may be under attack from someone (or about to be), but like the moment of an eclipse, when all is dark and it seems the world is ending, it will soon be over. Take care not to get involved in negative things; wait for this period to pass and then move on. Do not put too much pressure on the people around you in case you lose their support (Huang). In this situation, hold fast until this bad time burns itself out.

### Fourth line up

If you have this as a transforming line, someone is aiming negativity in your direction and that is causing others to think badly of you. Seek support from your loved ones and wait for the storm to pass. When the situation is clear again, you can relax and be less defensive. Pay special attention to those closest to you and strengthen your bonds with them (Gill). In this situation, stay with people you trust.

### Fifth line up

If you have this as a transforming line, there may be negativity in your life right now but this will soon be over. Make sure that those in power know the truth about you and guard against attack. Respect those who are as good as you or even better and tell them how proud you are of their capabilities (Huang). If you start to attract talented people to you, treat them well and use them correctly (Gill). Listen to everyone with respect (Adcock). In this situation, cultivate relationships with people of influence.

## Top line

If you have this as a transforming line, keep quiet about any good fortune you may be enjoying at this time. If you parade your ability, status or wealth you risk alienating people. In this situation, be humble even while your fire is burning bright.

# HEXAGRAM 56

**This hexagram represents: travel, wandering and the journey of life**

| | | Fire | | |
|---|---|---|---|---|
| 56 | | Li | | |
| | | Mountain | | |
| | | Gen | | |
| | 旅 | LU | | |

### READ ME FIRST

This hexagram appearing in your casting represents your "journey" through life. The lower trigram is **Mountain** and the upper trigram is **Fire**. The image is of fire spreading over the landscape as mountain vegetation burns in the hot, dry places of old China. Just as the fire goes where the wind blows, your progress is guided by the "winds of change".

**If you do not have any transforming lines:** focus on the things that really matter. Do not lose control of your emotions in this situation. Let go of trivial concerns and find happiness in the basics of life. If you let your emotions rage like a fire over a mountain, you will regret it.

**If you do have transforming lines:** consult those lines within this hexagram for a more direct answer. Then transform your hexagram and focus just on the **Read me first** section of the new hexagram to discover what you should do.

### Bottom line

If you have this as a transforming line, discard any petty problems. Do not let anything blow out of proportion. People will soon tire of you if you are a nuisance. In this situation, let go of the thing that is troubling you.

### Second line up

If you have this as a transforming line, you already have what you need to be happy or to achieve what you truly need to achieve. You also have the correct people around you, so do not look elsewhere. If you have the correct attitude toward life you will never be short of company and happiness. In this situation, stop searching; you already have everything you need.

### Third line up

If you have this as a transforming line, keep a calm head if things are getting difficult. If you take your frustration out on other people, they will think less of you and may even stop spending time with you. Find a positive way to release your stress. Treat people how you would want to be treated (Huang). If you find yourself alone in an unfamiliar setting, seek out like-minded friends (Crisp). In this situation, losing control of your emotions will not help.

### Fourth line up

If you have this as a transforming line, it means that you are looking beyond what you need. Appreciate what you have, even if your life is not filled with luxury. Having more will not necessarily make you happier. Alternatively, do not lower your guard (Crisp). If you are feeling unsettled, perhaps it is time to move on (Adcock). In this situation, count your blessings.

### Fifth line up

If you have this as a transforming line, now is a time to display your talents. Wherever your skills lie, show people what you can really do. If you do this, you may find life rewards you (Huang). In this situation, impress the people who need impressing.

### Top line

If you have this as a transforming line, help those who are in trouble. Their problems, if not resolved, may eventually become your problems. Take no notice if other people are mocking your misfortune; they will have their own problems one day. Always remember that you can create your own bad luck by being unkind to other people. In this situation, do what you can to help people in need.

## HEXAGRAM 57

**This hexagram represents: penetrating, moving along and calculation**

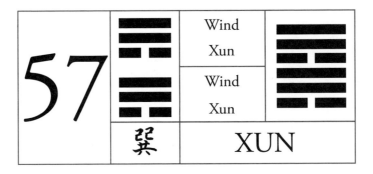

READ ME FIRST

This hexagram appearing in your casting means causing your ideas or thoughts to penetrate other people's minds. The lower and upper trigrams are both **Wind**. This is a difficult hexagram to encapsulate. Pearson uses the terms "compliance" and "choosing". She sees the two **Wind** trigrams together as a wind following another wind, showing how compliance and moving along should be a part of this reading. Huang agrees and adds that there is an element of humility involved here.

**If you do not have any transforming lines:** this hexagram is about capturing hearts and minds. Move softly and with ease. Apply gentle pressure and take your time to get what you want.

**If you do have transforming lines:** consult those lines within this hexagram for a more direct answer. Then transform your hexagram and focus just on the **Read me first** section of the new hexagram to discover what you should do.

## Bottom line

If you have this as a transforming line, you need to be resolute and decisive at this point. True determination will push you to the next stage (Huang). Remember that being gentle is not the same as being weak. A wind that blows softly for a long time is still a powerful force. In this situation, calm but constant pressure will work.

## Second line up

If you have this as a transforming line, call on religious ideas to get your point across. This could be by using common religious references that people will understand, or by appealing to people's spiritual beliefs to persuade them to open up to you and follow the path you want to tread. Equally, it could be that you need to reach into your own beliefs to discover the next path for yourself. Facing the divine, you should be humble and honest (Huang). Alternatively, avoid the superstitious and stick to reality (Gill). In this situation, find a way to encourage others by referring to higher principles.

## Third line up

If you have this as a transforming line, be warned that you should not try to persuade people too forcefully. Trying to impose your opinions will turn people's hearts against you. So, go easy. If you waver between two states or ideas while pretending to know what you are doing, people will be irritated (Huang). Do not dither like winds buffeting each other; move single-mindedly in one direction (Gill). If you focus only on what is bad you will remain stuck in the same place (Adcock). In this situation, present your ideas clearly and directly but without browbeating people.

## Fourth line up

If you have this as a transforming line, shrug off any setbacks. Do not dwell on mistakes, your own or others, and make a concerted effort to make a bad situation better. Let go of old problems, because if you do not move forward soon it will not be good for you (Crisp). In this situation, dust yourself off after a fall and get back into action right away.

## Fifth line up

If you have this as a transforming line, think before you act. If you decide that you still want to go ahead, do it. But avoid forcing the issue once you have made your move. Instead sit back and wait patiently for the results. In this situation, follow the formula of "sit and think, move and do, wait and see" so that you do not get ahead of yourself.

### Top line
If you have this as a transforming line, make sure that you are able to do what you say. If you make promises that you do not keep, it will not go well with the people around you. Decide whether you can actually achieve what you intend, but do not be discouraged if you cannot (Crisp and Gill). If you pay too much attention to trivial matters it will damage your overall position (Adcock). In this situation, take a reality check before you commit to anything.

## HEXAGRAM 58

**This hexagram represents: pleasing and joy**

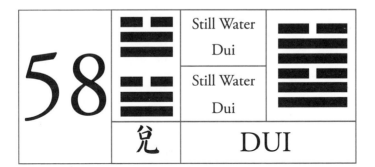

| 58 | ☱ | Still Water Dui | ☱ |
| | | Still Water Dui | |
| | 兑 | DUI | |

READ ME FIRST

This hexagram appearing in your casting relates to treating people in a way that will cause them to feel warmth and gratitude toward you. This may be something you do to repair a problem in a relationship. The lower and upper trigrams are both **Still Water**. The image is of two lakes connecting to share their water and other bounties with each other. Gill translates this hexagram as "the truth between friends that provides joy".

**If you do not have any transforming lines:** focus on politeness, hold no deception in your heart, do not pursue shallow aims, and act correctly. In this way, you will get where you need to get.

**If you do have transforming lines:** consult those lines within this hexagram for a more direct answer. Then transform your hexagram and focus just on the **Read me first** section of the new hexagram to discover what you should do.

### Bottom line
If you have this as a transforming line, you need to start communicating more openly with other people. Banish defensiveness and instead be warm and charming, polite and approachable. It is best in all cases to be in harmony with people, but do not take on their bad habits (Huang). Let go of any attachments to money or physical luxuries (Adcock). In this situation, warm relationships with other people are paramount.

### Second line up
If you have this as a transforming line, use sincerity to overcome any previous disagreements. Do not engage with people while holding deception or any kind of hidden agenda in your heart. In this situation, be open and honest and draw a line under any problems from the past

### Third line up
If you have this as a transforming line, it means you should not approach people in a shallow manner. Making false promises will cause more trouble than it is worth. Having too much of something can be as bad as not having enough (Crisp). If you chase joy or pleasure then you have missed the point (Gill). In this situation, pursuing shallow goals will take you far away from true joy.

### Fourth line up
If you have this as a transforming line, simply discussing an issue will not resolve it. You have to find the root of the problem. Go back to first principles to work out where to start. Also, do not just try to chase pleasure (Crisp). You cannot force happiness (Gill). Find purity in what you want (Adcock). In this situation, look for the correct action and not the correct words.

### Fifth line up

If you have this as a transforming line, be very careful what you say in public and who you confide in. There may be people around you who do not have your best interests at heart. Avoid shallow people-pleasers (Huang). Protect yourself by keeping your guard up at this time (Crisp). In this situation, look for the spy in your midst.

### Top line

If you have this as a transforming line, put the correct rewards in place to get the correct responses. People need to know what they will get for helping you. This does not mean they are greedy; they just want to be sure that their hard work will be recognized. Avoid falling under the influence of pleasure-seekers; what they are pursuing is false joy and not the real thing (Gill). If you become intoxicated by pleasure you will lose control (Adcock). In this situation, explain to people how they will benefit from supporting you.

## HEXAGRAM 59

**This hexagram represents: dispersing and dissolving**

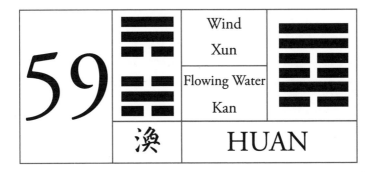

| 59 | | Wind<br>Xun | |
| | | Flowing Water | |
| | | Kan | |
| | 渙 | HUAN | |

READ ME FIRST

This hexagram appearing in your casting means that the situation may be dissipating and becoming unstable. The lower trigram is **Flowing Water** and the upper trigram is **Wind**. The image is of the wind dispersing water, such as when a strong gust blows droplets from a waterfall out into the air or causes the crests of waves to form spray.

**If you do not have any transforming lines:** reconnect with people because the elements of the situation are in the process of separating. You have to decide whether to try to restore stability, allow things to disperse as they will, or redistribute them purposefully.

**If you do have transforming lines:** consult those lines within this hexagram for a more direct answer. Then transform your hexagram and focus just on the **Read me first** section of the new hexagram to discover what you should do.

### Bottom line

If you have this as a transforming line, quickly put an end to any problems that are arising. If you do not attend to them now, they will get bigger. Pull together with others to get through this time. In this situation, deal with problems immediately.

### Second line up

If you have this as a transforming line, keep a calm head even if the situation around you is breaking down. You need to be a stable force at this time. Keep relaxed so that you relax others. Follow the rhythm of the moment (Huang). Decide which things are important to you and keep them close, but let everything else go (Gill). Do not judge others too harshly at this time (Adcock). If you feel out of place, leave the problem and find somewhere more comfortable (Crisp). In this situation, be a model of composure and stability for the people around you.

### Third line up

If you have this as a transforming line, approach people who have left the situation and respectfully ask them to return. It is time to knuckle down and save what you have been working for (Crisp). If you work for the benefit of others, you will reap the spiritual rewards (Gill). In this situation, bring lost sheep back into the fold, set to work and get what you want done.

### Fourth line up

If you have this as a transforming line, build up your supporters to help you get through. Make sure people see you as an individual and recognize you for your own merits (Crisp). Alternatively, it might be time to disband the group of people around you to clear the way for a better future (Gill). Consider letting go of short-term benefits to gain long-term rewards (Adcock). In this situation, decide whether to keep hold or let go.

### Fifth line up
If you have this as a transforming line, share your "wealth", whatever form it may take, with the people around you. This may be done to help those who are in need or as a reward for their support. Stick to your ideas, as they are better than the ones other people are putting forward (Crisp). Alternatively, if you are stuck maybe it is time to look for new ideas within the group (Adcock). In this situation, be generous with your resources, as this will bind your group closer to you.

### Top line
If you have this as a transforming line, you are having to pay a hefty price for success. What you are doing to achieve your goals is emotionally draining. If this is too much, give yourself some distance from the situation (Huang). It may be time to go it alone (Crisp and Gill). Make sure you and the people you are with stay away from negativity, whether it comes from within the group or without (Adcock). In this situation, weigh up how much you want it and whether it is worth the effort.

## HEXAGRAM 60

**This hexagram represents: regulation, limitation and control**

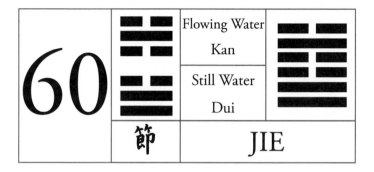

| 60 | Flowing Water Kan | |
| | Still Water Dui | |
| 節 | JIE | |

This hexagram appearing in your casting means you need to take control of the situation, as things are starting to get out of hand. The lower trigram is **Still Water** and the upper trigram is **Flowing Water**. The image is of the regulation of water. Water is dynamic and free flowing but it can be confined and controlled. However, when it breaks out of those parameters the results can be devastating.

**If you do not have any transforming lines:** things will spiral out of control if they carry on like this. Therefore, you need to regulate the situation and stop just aimlessly doing things. It is time to focus your efforts in a clear direction. However, make sure your focus is correct: do you want financial growth, spiritual growth or something else? The way you regulate yourself now will define the outcome.

**If you do have transforming lines:** consult those lines within this hexagram for a more direct answer. Then transform your hexagram and focus just on the **Read me first** section of the new hexagram to discover what you should do.

### Bottom line

If you have this as a transforming line, you need to curtail your outgoings because what you are giving out to the world, whether in terms of money, effort or time, is more than you can afford. Have restraint in all things (Huang) and focus on your own base camp (Gill). Avoid unnecessary risks at this time (Crisp). In this situation, it is time to accumulate not spend.

### Second line up

If you have this as a transforming line, now is not a time to focus on regulating your resources, you should take that gamble and go for it. Be less strict about how you manage your life, emotionally and physically. Get out of your comfort zone and engage with the world. If you do not act you may miss the crucial moment. In this situation, throw caution to the wind and take any opportunities that present themselves.

### Third line up

If you have this as a transforming line, look out for someone within your circle whose actions are having an adverse effect on you personally. Ask them to refrain from doing it. Also, if you do not set yourself restrictions than you will suffer misfortune (Gill). Find a balance between frugality and indulgence, as too much of either will lead to misery (Crisp). Know your limits and stick to them (Adcock). In this situation, regulate your own behaviour and that of people close to you.

## Fourth line up
If you have this as a transforming line, it is time to fully focus on your lifestyle and decide what you should store up and what you should give out. Balance your incomings and outgoings so that your resources grow overall. This should be a time of accumulation not a time of waste. If you want to succeed than you must place restrictions on yourself. Furthermore, do not fight against any limitations that have been put on you at the present, as they may be of benefit to you in the end. In this situation, balance your life so that it flows and grows.

## Fifth line up
If you have this as a transforming line, it is time to change your focus from material wealth to spiritual growth. You have cared too much about what you can get and not enough about what your spirit needs, but if you restrict your spending now you will nurture your spirit (Huang). It may be the time to take a tough decision to give up a lucrative activity (Gill). People will not stick to the rules if you do not set a good example (Adcock). In this situation, focus on what is best for your spirit not your bank balance.

## Top line
If you have this as a transforming line, it means that you should not push regulation or frugality too far. Penny-pinching or buttoning up your emotions will result in negativity. Therefore, ease the pressure and allow yourself to spend a bit more, financially, emotionally and spiritually. Too much determination brings its own problems (Huang) and too many restrictions will trap you (Gill). It is also good to moderate your moderation (Crisp). In this situation, loosen up.

# HEXAGRAM 61

**This hexagram represents: trust and mutual respect**

| 61 | | Wind<br>Xun | |
| | | Still Water<br>Dui | |
| | 中孚 | ZHONG FU | |

This hexagram appearing in your casting means that mutual trust and openness between all people needs to be reached. The lower trigram is **Still Water** and the upper trigram is **Wind**. The image is of wind rippling the still surface of a lake. The wind and the water meet in the middle, just as people do when they interact with each other. Like wind, sincere and heartfelt friendship cannot be seen but it is felt strongly.

**If you do not have any transforming lines:** mutual benefit and understanding is the key to success here. Find group harmony and encourage those who may be a little afraid to step up and join you.

**If you do have transforming lines:** consult those lines within this hexagram for a more direct answer. Then transform your hexagram and focus just on the **Read me first** section of the new hexagram to discover what you should do.

### Bottom line

If you have this as a transforming line, make sure that you are not hiding any traps within your plan. If you are trying to deceive someone, think again. It is best to be open and honest at this time. If you want something more than mutual benefit and wish to profit over others, it will not work (Huang). Alternatively, depending too much on others could be a weakness in your strategy (Crisp). Do not follow other people, stick to your own ways (Adcock). In this situation, make sure all parties will benefit from what you are proposing.

### Second line up

If you have this as a transforming line, foster mutual trust by demonstrating the rewards available to those who work with you. Coax people out of their defensive position by being open and honest. Be clear with your feelings and others will come to you (Crisp and Adcock). In this situation, show others that they can trust you.

### Third line up

If you have this as a transforming line, something has happened to jeopardize the mutual trust you share with someone else. Be careful, because what you do at this point could either repair or sever this relationship. If you want to avoid a loss, you must remain totally honest at this time (Huang). Furthermore, do not rely on other people too much. In this situation, rebuild trust through transparency.

### Fourth line up

If you have this as a transforming line, guard against someone – possibly someone close – who may be trying to deceive you. Alternatively, look to those who inspire you and bond with them (Crisp). If things are going well at this stage do not forget who helped you get to this position (Adcock). In this situation, make sure you are getting what you need and that no one is trying to deceive you.

### Fifth line up

If you have this as a transforming line, success comes from relying on your friends and family, the most trusted people you know. Do not look elsewhere. If you lie to yourself you will project a negative aura and people will pick up on that and withdraw their support (Gill); but if you have a strong inner truth, people will follow you (Adcock). In this situation, turn to those you trust to help you get what you need.

### Top line

If you have this as a transforming line, now is time to stop talking and start doing. You will never sprout wings, no matter how much you boast about your plans to fly. Therefore, just keep quiet and move into action.

Alternatively, make yourself heard and your intentions clear (Crisp). Take heed of warnings, as ignoring them will bring misfortune (Gill). Lead the way in all things (Adcock). In this situation, move forward with quiet determination.

## HEXAGRAM 62

**This hexagram represents: small matters, lesser challenges and staying within yourself**

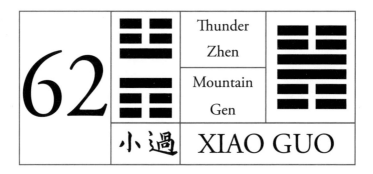

| 62 | | Thunder Zhen | |
|---|---|---|---|
| | | Mountain Gen | |
| | 小過 | XIAO GUO | |

READ ME FIRST

This hexagram appearing in your casting means that you should focus on the smaller parts of a problem and leave the bigger aspects for now. Do not go beyond where you are safe and comfortable. The lower trigram is **Mountain** and the upper trigram is **Thunder**. The image here is of a warning not to climb too far up the mountain. The higher you rise, the closer you will get to the storm. Be realistic about your abilities and do not go beyond them.

**If you do not have any transforming lines:** tidy up all the little loose ends that have been hanging around before they escalate into bigger problems. Do not overreach at this time.

**If you do have transforming lines:** consult those lines within this hexagram for a more direct answer. Then transform your hexagram and focus just on the **Read me first** section of the new hexagram to discover what you should do.

## Bottom line

If you have this as a transforming line, do not take on things that are too much for you. You may want to do something, but can you pull it off? Restraint at this time is the best policy (Huang). Bide your time at the moment (Adcock). In this situation, be realistic about your abilities.

## Second line up

If you have this as a transforming line, this is a time for you to take on extra responsibilities. Few people want to add to their work load, but this will be a positive thing for you. It will show people your abilities and result in success in the end. Trying to get around the problem will not work (Crisp). Instead, work directly with the person who is involved in the situation (Gill). For the time being, be satisfied with any small progress you make along the path to your goal (Adcock). In this situation, be happy with small steps and make yourself available for any extra work that is needed.

## Third line up

If you have this as a transforming line, be careful not to do the wrong thing, as this will turn out badly for you. Stick with what you know. Watch out for any hidden attacks people may make on you (Crisp and Gill). Now is a time for caution (Adcock). In this situation, play it safe.

## Fourth line up

If you have this as a transforming line, try to find a way around the problem if you can but if this is not possible just do not push it, as this will get you nowhere. Be careful not to overreact in any situations you may encounter (Huang). At this time, create a solid fort around you so no one can attack you. In this situation, do not force the issue at this time.

## Fifth line up

If you have this as a transforming line, things are not as bad as they seem. You can change an unpromising situation into a good one. Take small steps and approach the moment with the aim of resolving all issues. Find people to support you at this time (Crisp). Any help, no matter how small, will be welcome. In this situation, change a negative to a positive.

## Top line

If you have this as a transforming line, you need to deal with the situation directly and positively and without escalating the matter. You cannot solve the problem by going around it or getting other people to come in and help. Focus on the details at this point (Crisp). Do not leave the safety of a strong position; now is not the time to try anything beyond your means or ability (Gill and Adcock). In this situation, solve the larger problem by dealing directly with all the smaller issues.

# HEXAGRAM 63

**This hexagram represents: accomplishments and partial success**

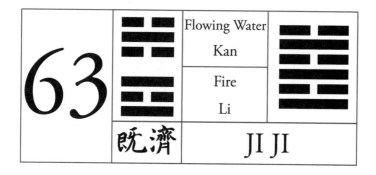

| 63 | Flowing Water Kan | |
| | Fire Li | |
| | 既濟 | JI JI |

READ ME FIRST

This hexagram appearing in your casting means that you have got a certain way toward achieving your intended goal already, but there may be some further small problems or small steps which you need to overcome or take. The lower trigram is **Fire** and the upper trigram is **Flowing Water**. The image is of a fire burning away in full heat, yet water hangs above it ready to douse the flames. It means that you are not at the finish line, but neither are you at the start.

**If you do not have any transforming lines:** you may be in a good position, even a better position than you think. But be careful: if you make a wrong move now it could destroy all you have achieved. Huang disagrees with this assessment, seeing the hexagram as a reflection of the idea in Chinese thought that things need to move in the direction that is natural to them.

Water naturally flows downward and heat rises, making this hexagram one where everything is set up for proper movement. The fire is rising and heating the water so that tea can be made. Everything is in the right place and progress is being made, but there is work still to be done.

**If you do have transforming lines:** consult those lines within this hexagram for a more direct answer. Then transform your hexagram and focus just on the **Read me first** section of the new hexagram to discover what you should do.

### Bottom line
If you have this as a transforming line, any issues you are having at this moment will not affect your overall goal. Push on through them. Do not let any success you have had go to your head or cause you to make bad decisions; keep a restrained mind (Crisp). Be careful what you do, as your actions now will have a ripple effect later on (Huang). In this situation, do not let past successes or current setbacks push you off course.

### Second line up
If you have this as a transforming line, do not fret if you have had a setback or lost something close to you, be it physical or emotional. This is just a temporary problem and things will return to their correct balance. You may be overlooked now, but your rewards will not be held back forever (Crisp). In this situation, take the hit and keep fighting.

### Third line up
If you have this as a transforming line, make sure you do not allow incapable people to slow your progress. You have made some progress toward your goal, so be careful that what you do now does not get in the way. Take any measures that are needed to stop other people blocking you (Huang). Also, at this stage of your progress remind everyone involved of the rules and regulations you are working within and the goals you are striving for (Crisp). If you drop your personal standards now that you have tasted some success you will fall back down to where you started (Adcock). If people start demanding anything from you, do not give it to them (Gill). In this situation, maintain discipline and standards to protect what you have achieved and keep you on course for what remains to be done.

### Fourth line up

If you have this as a transforming line, putting too much faith in people at this stage may hamper your progress. Without causing offence, keep control of the situation and do the job yourself. You may be doing well now, but be prepared for times in the future when things are not so great. Use any problems to identify weaknesses in the current set-up and prevent future failures (Adcock). In this situation, protect yourself against future problems by learning from current ones and accepting the natural cycle of highs and lows.

### Fifth line up

If you have this as a transforming line, you may not have the power to achieve your goals yet. That being so, you should push your resources of talent, energy and money to the limit you have allowed for this venture. Now is the time to make a sacrifice to get yourself to the next level. Do not worry that what you are giving is not enough; if it is given in true kindness it will be well received (Crisp). Keep things straight and simple (Adcock). In this situation, put in as much as you can without burning yourself out; even if it does not get you all the way, your effort will be rewarded.

### Top line

If you have this as a transforming line, you do not have to worry one bit about any opponent or difficult situation. You have already won and gained what you need, even if you do not realize it yet. Take another look, you may be in a better position than you think. Gather your energy for the next stage of your journey (Huang). Look to the future, not the past (Crisp and Adcock). Make sure to pay full attention to the situation (Gill). In this situation, there may be further to go but you should recognize just how far you have come already.

# HEXAGRAM 64

**This hexagram represents: not there yet and transition**

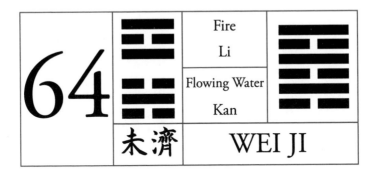

| 64 | | Fire<br>Li | |
| | | Flowing Water<br>Kan | |
| | 未濟 | WEI JI | |

**READ ME FIRST**

This hexagram appearing in your casting means that you have not achieved all that you want to achieve and you are not likely to do so at this time. The lower trigram is **Flowing Water** and the upper trigram is **Fire**. The image contains elements that cannot move and so are stagnant. Fire is at the top so the heat cannot rise further, while water is at the bottom so there is nowhere for it to flow. This is a time for reflection, self-improvement and perseverance.

**If you do not have any transforming lines:** achieving your goal is not an option right now, but you can still equip yourself for future success. Take time out, relax, train your mind and body in the skills you need. Find a model to aspire to, so you can become the person you need to be to achieve what you want to do.

**If you do have transforming lines:** consult those lines within this hexagram for a more direct answer. Then transform your hexagram and focus just on the **Read me first** section of the new hexagram to discover what you should do.

**Bottom line**

If you have this as a transforming line, it means that you have not yet accomplished your objective, and at this time you will not be able to. Use this period to prepare and train yourself for the next part of your journey. Focus on self-improvement. If you try to go beyond your ability you will fail (Crisp) and it will be a humiliation (Gill). Know the difference between correct effort and going too far (Huang) and do not be impulsive (Adcock). In this situation, you cannot progress now but you can prepare yourself for future challenges.

### Second line up

If you have this as a transforming line, play it safe and wait for the next opening. Stop and wait because if you go too fast things will fall apart (Gill). Now is a time for preparation, so you do not need to stand still even though you cannot move forward (Adcock). Also, do not strut about showing off (Huang). In this situation, it is best to wait but use the time constructively.

### Third line up

If you have this as a transforming line, your goal is going to be very difficult to achieve right now, but not impossible. You have a long and difficult road ahead, so ask yourself if you want to keep going or not. If the answer is yes, enlist people to help you move on to the next stage (Crisp), because you are only part of the way there (Gill). In this situation, prepare yourself for a long, hard slog.

### Fourth line up

If you have this as a transforming line, pay attention to what your rivals or superiors are doing. Learn from those who are better than you at what you want to achieve. Be bold in your actions (Crisp). You are on the right path (Gill), so sustain your correct attitude (Huang). In this situation, find a role model and emulate their approach.

### Fifth line up

If you have this as a transforming line, show people how committed to the issue you are. You may have a long way to go, but inspiring people's confidence in you now will help at a later point. Share your time, energy, emotions or resources with all those who support you (Gill). In this situation, let people see that you have what it takes.

## Top line
If you have this as a transforming line, it is important not to overindulge in anything. This could be food, drink, emotions, leisure, work and so on. Losing your overall focus will cause problems. In this situation, find a balance between all the different aspects of your life.

# ABOUT THE AUTHOR

Antony Cummins is the Official Tourism Ambassador for Wakayama, Japan (和歌山市観光発信人) and the author of an array of books on historical Asian military culture, specifically Japanese. His intention is to present a historically accurate picture of both samurai and *shinobi* (ninja) to the western world and lay down the foundations for a better understanding of their teachings and ways. He has also written books on influential Chinese traditions, including *The Ultimate Art of War* and *The Ultimate Guide to Yin Yang* (both Watkins). For more information see his website, www.natori.co.uk.

# ABOUT THE GRAPHIC DESIGNER

Jayson Kane is a Manchester-based graphic designer and illustrator, otherwise known as Kane Kong Illustrates (@kanekongillustrates on instagram). He studied Art, Design and Print Making, specializing in Visual Communication. Having worked with Antony Cummins for many years, his portfolio includes: *True Path of the Ninja* (cover concept design), *The Secret Traditions of the Shinobi* (front cover design), *Iga and Koka Ninja Skills* (internal illustrations), *The Illustrated Guide to Viking Martial Arts* (internal illustrations), *Ninja Skills* (internal illustrations), *Old Japan* (internal illustrations), *Modern Ninja Warfare* (internal illustrations), *The Old Stones* (internal diagrams), *The Ultimate Art of War* (internal illustrations) and *How to Be a Modern Samurai* (internal illustrations).

# BIBLIOGRAPHY

Adcock, W., *How to Use the I-Ching*. Lorenz Books, London, 2015.

Allinson, R. E. (editor), *Understanding the Chinese Mind: The Philosophical Roots*. Oxford University Press, Hong Kong, 1989.

Chan, W., *A Sourcebook in Chinese Philosophy*. Princeton University Press, Princeton, NJ, 1963.

Chen, Y., "Legitimation Discourse and the Theory of the Five Elements in Imperial China", *Journal of Song-Yuan Studies*, Volume 44. Society for Song, Yuan and Conquest Dynasty Studies, 2014.

Crisp, P., *The Little Book of Changes: A Pocket I-Ching*. Mandala Publishing, San Rafael, CA, 2012.

Cummins, A., *The Ultimate Guide to Yin Yang: An Illustrated Exploration of the Chinese Concept of Opposites*. Watkins, London, 2021.

Gill, R., *I Ching: The Little Book That Tells the Truth*. Aquarian Press, 1990.

Herman, J., *Taoism for Dummies*. John Wiley & Sons, New York, 2013.

Huang, A., *The Complete I Ching: The Definitive Translation*. Inner Traditions, Rochester, VT, 1998.

Huang, A., *Understanding the I Ching: Restoring a Brilliant, Ancient Culture*. CreateSpace Independent Publishing Platform, 2014.

Karcher, S., *How to Use the I Ching: A Guide to Working with the Oracle of Change*. Element Books, Shaftesbury, Dorset, 1997.

Lai, K., *An Introduction to Chinese Philosophy*. Cambridge University Press, Cambridge, 2008.

Lai, K., *Learning from Chinese Philosophies: Ethics of Interdependent and Contextualised Self*. Ashgate, Farnham, Surrey, 2006.

Leaman, O., *Encyclopedia of Asian Philosophy*. Routledge, London, 2001.

Leibniz, G.W. (author), D.J. Cook and H. Rosemont, Jr. (translators and editors), *Writings on China*. Open Court Books, Chicago and LaSalle, IL, 1994.

Liu, J., *An Introduction to Chinese Philosophy: From Ancient Philosophy to Chinese Buddhism*. Blackwell Books, Oxford, 2006.

MacNicol, W., *The Cup of Knowledge: A Key to the Mysteries of Divination*. J. & B. Dodsworth Ltd, UK, 1924.

Moran, E. and Yu, J., *The Complete Idiot's Guide to the I Ching*. DK Books, 2001.

Pearson, M. J., *The Original I-Ching: An Authentic Translation of the Book of Changes Based on Recent Discoveries*. Tuttle, North Clarendon, VT, 2011.

Rochat de la Vallée, E., *The Five Elements in Chinese Classical Texts*. Monkey Press, UK, 2009.

Rochat de la Vallée, E., *Yin Yang in Classical Texts*. Monkey Press, UK, 2006.

Rudd, R., *The Gene Keys: Embracing Your Higher Purpose*. Watkins, London, 2013.

Schwartz, B. I., *The World of Thought in Ancient China*. Belknap Press, Cambridge, MA, 1985.

Stepaniants, M., *Introduction to Eastern Thought*. AltaMira Press, Walnut Creek, CA, 2002.

Tai, S., *Principles of Feng Shui: An Illustrated Guide to Chinese Geomancy*. Asiapac Books, Singapore, 1998.

Wang R. R., *Yinyang: The Way of Heaven and Earth in Chinese Thought and Culture*. Cambridge University Press, Cambridge, 2012.

Weatherstone, L., *I-Ching: 64 Oracle Cards*. Lo Scarabeo, Turin, Italy, 2017.

Wilhelm, R., *The Secret of the Golden Flower: A Chinese Book of Life*. Harcourt, Brace & Co., New York, 1931.

# INDEX

Note: page numbers in **bold** refer to illustrations, page numbers in *italics* refer to information contained in tables.